ESSENTIAL ELEMENTS 2000

COMPREHENSIVE BAND METHOD

TIM LAUTZENHEISER
PAUL LAVENDER

JOHN HIGGINS
TOM C. RHODES

CHARLES MENGHINI
DON BIERSCHENK

Percussion consultant and editor
WILL RAPP

Dear Music Educator,

Welcome to *Essential Elements 2000, Book 2*. The following pages offer an ongoing sequential-learning curriculum, PLUS a library of additional benefits certain to offer every student a positive pathway to musical excellence.

In addition to the many popular features from *Essential Elements, Book 1*, this second book offers new exciting opportunities for teachers. The Individual Study section features etudes which explore useful techniques that are unique to each instrument. These are followed by a special solo with written piano accompaniment from the Rubank® library of solos. And, on the Play-Along CD Disc 1 (included in every student book), these etudes and solos are demonstrated by a professional soloist with classical piano accompaniments. See the section USING ESSENTIAL ELEMENTS 2000 for more details on the features of this book.

Throughout our series, there is a reinforcement of the National Standards for Arts Education including music theory, history, improvisation, and composition. Our team of authors has carefully designed every aspect of *Essential Elements 2000* to support the important academic value of music as a core subject in our schools.

We are delighted that you and your students have chosen *Essential Elements 2000* as your musical companion. Please accept our best wishes as you STRIKE UP THE BAND!

Sincerely,

Tim Lautzenheiser

MUSIC, an essential element of life.

ISBN 0-634-01238-X

Copyright © 2000 by HAL LEONARD CORPORATION
International Copyright Secured   All Rights Reserved

HAL•LEONARD®
CORPORATION
7777 W. BLUEMOUND RD. P.O. BOX 13819 MILWAUKEE, WI 53213

2

TABLE OF CONTENTS

Student Page	Topic/Title	Conductor Page

4

SEQUENCE OF

Director Page	1	12–17	18–23	24–30	31–37	38–45	46–50	51–56	57–61	62–68	69–74	75–81
Student Page	**1**	**2**	**3**	**4**	**5**	**6**	**7**	**8**	**9**	**10**	**11**	**12**
Rhythms										Cut Time Syncopation $\sharp\sharp \; \sharp = \sharp\sharp \; \sharp$ $\frac{2}{4}$ $\mathbb{C}$	Sixteenth Notes	
Theory							Key Changes	$\mathbb{C}$ or $\frac{2}{2}$	Syncopation	Key Signature: Concert C		
History						Tallis Canon		Loch Lomond	Cohen			
Terms						Staccato / Tenuto / Sightreading S–T–A–R–S	Ritardando, Allegretto	Dynamics: *cresc., decresc.*	Dynamics: *mp*			
Special Features	Play Along CD Disc 1, 2, 3	Book 1 Review	Book 1 Review	Book 1 Review	Round, Sightreading Challenge	Daily Warm-Ups	Sightreading Challenge	Essential Creativity: $\mathbb{C}$ writing assignment		Sightreading Challenge	Duet	Perf. Spotlight, Band Arr.: *Chorale, The Thunderer, Hill and Gully Rider, Shenandoah*
Quiz Objectives								Pick-ups, Accents, Syncopation, Dynamics, Accidentals,			16ths, Accents, Syncopation, Counting Rests	
Note Sequence												
Flute												
Oboe												
B♭ Clarinet B♭ Bass Clar.					Cl. only					Right Hand		
E♭ Alto Clar.												
E♭ Alto Sax. E♭ Bar. Sax.												
B♭ T. Sax.												
B♭ Trumpet Bar. T.C.												
F Horn												
Trombone Bar. B.C. Bassoon E. Bass												
Tuba												
Kybd. Perc.												
Percussion Techniques						Flam Paradiddle Bass Drum Roll	Drag					
New Perc. Instruments					Temple Blocks						Tom-Tom Drum Set	Bongos
Correlating Band Arr. Levels												

ESSENTIAL ELEMENTS

Director Page	82–87	88–93	94–98	99–104	105–109	110–115	116–124	125–130	131–135	136–140	141–146	147–152
Student Page	**13**	**14**	**15**	**16**	**17**	**18**	**19**	**20**	**21**	**22**	**23**	**24**
Rhythms		♫	♫		♫			¢ ♩. ♪ = ²/₄ ♫				♫³
Theory		Key Signature: Concert A♭							**6/8**	Enharmonics, Chromatics		Triplets
History						Bizet	Advance Australia Fare	Sousa		Habañera		
Terms	D.S. al Fine	A♭ Concert Scale		Rallentando			Enharmonics, E♭ Concert Scale, A Tempo			Chromatic Scale		
Special Features	Perf. Spotlight Band Arr.: *Las Mañanitas, Rondeau, Rock.com*			Duet, Sightreading Challenge	Trio	Daily Warm-Ups	Essential Creativity: Arrange America	Sightreading Challenge			Sightreading Challenge	Duet
Quiz Objectives			♫, ♫ D.C. al Fine Dynamics Key, Slurs						**6/8** Rhythms, Dynamics			♫³ Key, Articulations

Note Sequence

Flute		♭♩					Enharmonic ♭♩ ♮♯					
Oboe												
B♭ Clarinet B♭ Bass Clar.		Cl. only ♭♩ Left Hand					Enharmonic ♭♩ ♮♯	Right Hand		Left Hand ♯♭♯♭ Chromatic		
E♭ Alto Clar.		♭♩					♩					
E♭ Alto Sax. E♭ Bar. Sax.		♭♩					Enharmonic ♩ ♭♩ ♮♯					
B♭ T. Sax.							Enharmonic ♭♩ ♮♯			Alt. fingering ♯♭		
B♭ Trumpet Bar. T.C.		♭♩					Enharmonic ♩ ♭♩ ♮♯					
F Horn												
Trombone Bar. B.C. Bassoon E. Bass		♭♩					♭♩					
Tuba		♭♩					♭♩					
Kybd. Perc.							Enharmonic ♭♩ ♮♯					

Percussion Techniques

Percussion Techniques	Cross Stick Rim Shot	Tambourine Knee to Fist Technique; Flam Rudiment Review; Crash Cymbal Chokes	Tambourine Sixteenth Note Technique			R R L L Double Bounce			Multiple Bounce in **6/8**	Tambourine Thumb Roll		
New Perc. Instruments	Guiro						Timbales					

| **Correlating Band Arr. Levels** | | | ▲ Expert Level | | | | | | | | | |

SEQUENCE OF

Director Page	153–159	160–164	165–171	172–179	180–187	188–193	194–207	208–219	220–231	232–238	239–246	247–253
Student Page	**25**	**26**	**27**	**28**	**29**	**30**	**31**	**32**	**33**	**34**	**35**	**36**
Rhythms	♩. ♫			♪ ♩ ♪ / ♩ ♫ ♫ ♩								
Theory						Major and Minor						
History		The Marines Hymn	Waltz									
Terms	F Concert Scale	D.S. al Fine, Accelerando	Andantino, Legato style	Measure Repeat ％		Natural Minor Scale, Harmonic Minor Scale	D.S. al Coda					
Special Features							Perf. Spotlight Band Arr.: *Simple Gifts, Semper Fidelis*	Perf. Spotlight Band Arr.: *Danny Boy, Take Me Out To the Ballgame*	Perf. Spotlight Band Arr.: *Serengeti*	Rubank ® Studies	Rubank ® Studies	Rubank ® Studies
Quiz Objectives	(rhythm figures) Dynamics		Pick-up, Repeats, Dynamics, 16th notes, Slurs									
Note Sequence — Flute	(notation)											
Oboe	(notation)											
B♭ Clarinet / B♭ Bass Clar.	(notation)					Cl. only (notation)						
E♭ Alto Clar.	(notation)											
E♭ Alto Sax. / E♭ Bar. Sax.	(notation)											
B♭ T. Sax.	(notation)											
B♭ Trumpet / Bar. T.C.	(notation)					Bar. T.C. only (notation)						
F Horn	(notation)											
Trombone / Bar. B.C. / Bassoon / E. Bass	(notation)					(– E. Bass) (notation)						
Tuba	(notation)					(notation)						
Kybd. Perc.	(notation)											
Percussion Techniques			Natural Sticking	R R L L Flam Tap	³ Sixteenth Note Triplet		Open Rolls in 6/8					
New Perc. Instruments	Hi-Hat			Congas	Chimes				Wind Chimes			
Correlating Band Arr. Levels							▲ Master Level					

ESSENTIAL ELEMENTS

Director Page	254–261	262–281	262–281	262–281	262–281	282	283	284–290	291	292–329	292–329	330–331
Student Page	**37**	**38**	**39**	**40**	**41**	**42**	**43**	**44**	**45**	**46**	**47**	**48**
Rhythms												
Theory								Theme and Variation, Blues Improvisation				
History												
Terms		Clarinet: Alt. Fingerings Reference Chart		Clarinet: Grace Notes								
Special Features	Rubank® Studies	Individual Study	Individual Study	Individual Study Solo	Individual Study Piano Acc.	Rhythm Studies	Rhythm Studies	Creating Music	Essential Elements Star Achiever Chart	Fingering Chart Perc.: Rudiment Chart	Fingering Chart Perc.: Rudiment Chart	Reference Index
Quiz Objectives												

Note Sequence

Flute		
Oboe		
B♭ Clarinet / B♭ Bass Clar.		
E♭ Alto Clar.	Left Hand	
E♭ Alto Sax. / E♭ Bar. Sax.		
B♭ T. Sax.		
B♭ Trumpet / Bar. T.C.	Bar. T.C. only	
F Horn		
Trombone / Bar. B.C. / Bassoon / E. Bass	Bn. only	
Tuba		
Kybd. Perc.		
Percussion Techniques	L R L R R L L R L R R L Pataflafla	
New Perc. Instruments		

USING ESSENTIAL ELEMENTS 2000

ESSENTIAL ELEMENTS 2000 is a comprehensive method for beginning band musicians, and can be used with full band, like-instrument classes, or individuals. It is designed with fail-safe options for teachers to customize the learning program to meet their changing needs.

The Conductor book includes all the music and text from the student books, plus time-saving **EE Teaching Tips** throughout the score. As in the student books, the introduction of a new concept is always highlighted by a **color** box.

PLAY-ALONG CD DISC 1

Every student receives a play-along CD in their book which covers the first 55 exercises, plus the **Individual Study** section on student pages 38–41. Melodies are demonstrated by a small band ensemble in the first 55 exercises. However, these CDs are unique for each instrument; the Individual Study exercises and solos are recorded by a professional soloist playing **each specific instrument!**

For classroom use, the Conductor book includes a play-along CD featuring the first 55 exercises. Each track is played twice—the second time is the accompaniment track alone. There is a one measure count-off before each track.

Also available: *Play-Along CD Set, Disc 2 & 3 (ex. 56 to the end), and Play-Along CD Set, Disc 2 & 3 For Percussion.*

PERCUSSION

The 96-page Percussion book takes a **complete percussion** approach. Each regular student page is expanded to a 2-page spread which includes the **optional auxiliary percussion** parts and clear playing instructions for all instruments. The next 48 pages are the complete **Keyboard Percussion** parts. The student books include 2 Play-Along CDs; one features all the percussion including drums and auxiliaries, while the other demonstrates all keyboard parts.

On pages 322–350, look for special **EE Teaching Tips** which relate solely to Percussion.

INDIVIDUAL STUDY SECTION

There are specially designed individual instrument studies on pages 38–41 of each student book. The solo etudes explore useful techniques that are commonly associated with each instrument such as alternate fingerings, lip slurs, etc.

These etudes are followed by a carefully chosen solo with written piano accompaniment from the long-respected Rubank® library of solos. The etudes and solos also appear on the Play-Along CD Disc 1 in each student book, and feature a professional soloist accompanied by a classical pianist.

PRE-PLANNED CONCERT

ESSENTIAL ELEMENTS 2000 includes a complete pre-planned concert program on student pages 12–13. The material is flexible in design, featuring a warm-up chorale, a march, pieces to feature the woodwind, brass and percussion sections, an encore-style piece, etc.

The concert for parents could also include highlights of the music learned earlier in the year, as well as demonstrations of the instrument families. It can be successfully combined with Book 1's pre-planned concert material, featuring your beginning students as well.

The music on these 2 pages can also be used as a culmination activity to test or review all previously learned skills.

PERFORMANCE SPOTLIGHTS

In addition to the pre-planned concert, there are 5 more **full band arrangements** on student pages 31–33. Plus, the **duets** and **trio** can be used as ensembles or played by the full band. Performances for relatives, community organizations, or for the school itself are highly encouraged.

Refer to the Individual Study section for a **solo with written piano accompaniment** for each instrument. These solos are specially chosen for individual instruments from the time-tested Rubank® library.

RHYTHM RAPS

New rhythms are presented as clapping exercises in the innovative **Rhythm Rap** format. After each Rhythm Rap, the identical rhythms are played on simple pitches in the next exercise. Finally, they appear in an appropriate melodic setting in the subsequent (3rd) exercise.

DAILY WARM-UPS

You can establish good practice habits with this systematic approach for developing tone and technique. Use the Daily Warm-Ups on student page 18, replacing them with the second set of warm-ups when the class reaches page 30. In addition to tone and technique exercises, each includes a Bach chorale with simple harmony.

RUBANK® STUDIES

Developed from classic Rubank etudes, these supplemental exercises on student pages 34–37 provide many different teaching opportunities. They are excellent for expanding individual technical skills, and may be introduced as extra challenges when appropriate for individual players or sections.

These pages can also be used as full band **warm-ups** and **technique builders**. Included are warm-up chorales, scales and etudes in 5 major keys, scales and etudes in 3 minor keys, and 2 chromatic scales. Additional performance skills can be reinforced by varying the tempo, dynamics, etc.

EE RHYTHM STUDIES

These supplementary rhythm exercises appear on student pages 42–43. The rhythms advance sequentially, and can be used in any length of measure groupings. Simply choose the beginning and ending measure, plus any repetition desired.

Start by using a single pitch throughout the measure(s) selected. Then change pitch only at the beginning of measures. By specifying different times to change pitch, the rhythms can be very challenging.

MUSIC THEORY, HISTORY, AND CROSS-CURRICULAR ACTIVITIES

All the necessary materials to relate music to history, world cultures or other subjects are woven into the learning program—right in the student books. These Theory and History features are highlighted by **color** boxes and appear throughout the Book.

As a result, teachers can efficiently meet and exceed the **National Standards for Arts Education**, while still having the time to focus on music performance skills.

CREATIVITY

Essential Creativity exercises appear in several places (culminating on student page 44). They are designed to stimulate imaginations and to foster a creative attitude toward music. By completing the activities, students are guided through basic concepts about *Composition and Improvisation*.

ASSESSMENT

On student page 45, there is a complete list of 28 **Star Achiever** exercises. These include the Essential Elements Quiz and Creativity exercises, Sightreading Challenges, Performance Spotlights and additional lines which encompass all the notes and skills used in Book 2. On the students' page, they can fill in a star for each item which they pass.

Teachers can use this basic checklist to keep track of student performance assessments. In addition, there is a detailed list of items to evaluate **(EE QUIZ ASSESSMENTS)** above each quiz in the Conductor score. Each of these indicate all the new material and skills taught since the previous quiz.

Additional Resources Available...

PLAY-ALONG CD SET DISC 2 & 3

This set of play-along tracks includes exercise 56 through the end of Book 2. It features the melody demonstrated by a small band ensemble, followed by the accompaniment-only for each exercise. For use by all wind instruments. Also available: *Play-Along CD Set, Disc 2 & 3 For Percussion*.

TEACHER RESOURCE KIT

This valuable resource features assessment and enrichment materials plus a convenient set of lesson plans. A *CD-ROM* (Windows/Mac) with editable word processing files is also included.

PIANO ACCOMPANIMENT BOOK

Easy piano accompaniments for all the exercises.

CORRELATED MATERIALS

The ESSENTIAL ELEMENTS BAND SERIES includes original and popular music, arranged for younger bands. Each publication is correlated to one of five specific "levels" within Books 1 and 2 (see the Sequence Of Essential Elements chart in the Conductor book for details). Contact your music dealer or the publisher for information on the latest releases in this series.

REVIEW

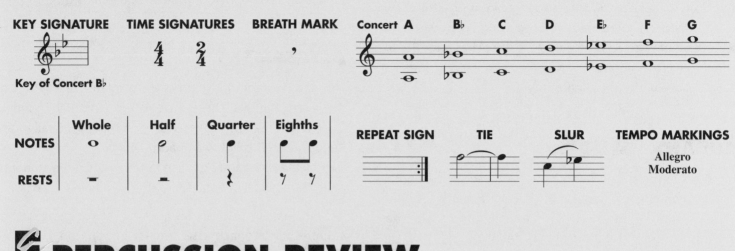

PERCUSSION REVIEW

TEACHING TIP Have students identify the *clef, key signature, time signature, repeat sign,* and *breath mark.*

1. TECHNIQUE TRAX

 **TEACHING TIP** Review the 2/4 *time signature, tied notes,
quarter rest,* and the definition of **Allegro**.

2. SHOO FLY

American Folk Song

14

🎵 **TEACHING TIP**   Review *eighth notes, slurred notes,* and the definition of **Moderato**.
Have the students count and finger this exercise before playing.

3. THAILAND LULLABY

Thai Folk Song

 **TEACHING TIP** Keep fingers in a good position over the keys or valves to play the slurred notes steady and clean. The trombone slide should move quickly with fast air.

4. SHEPHERD'S HEY

English Folk Song

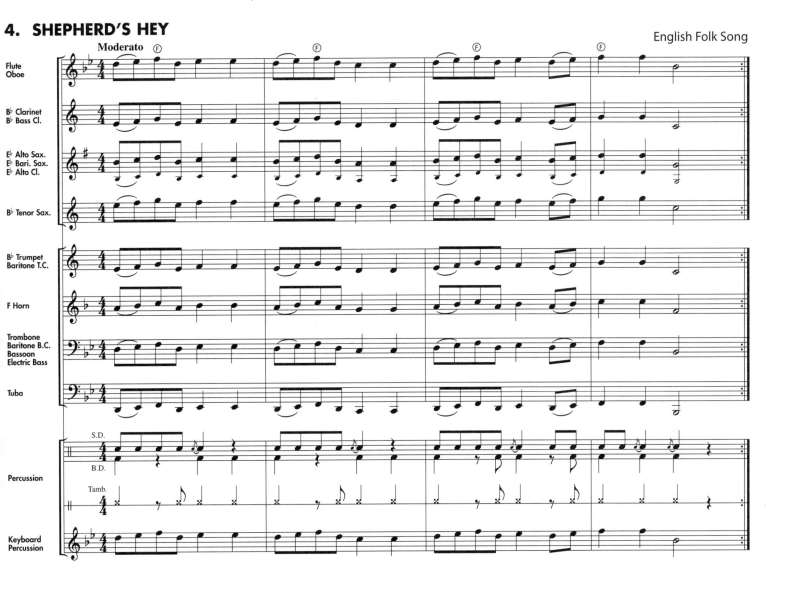

✦ **TEACHING TIP**   Review *half rests* and *whole rests*.

5. THE CRAWDAD SONG

American Folk Song

REVIEW

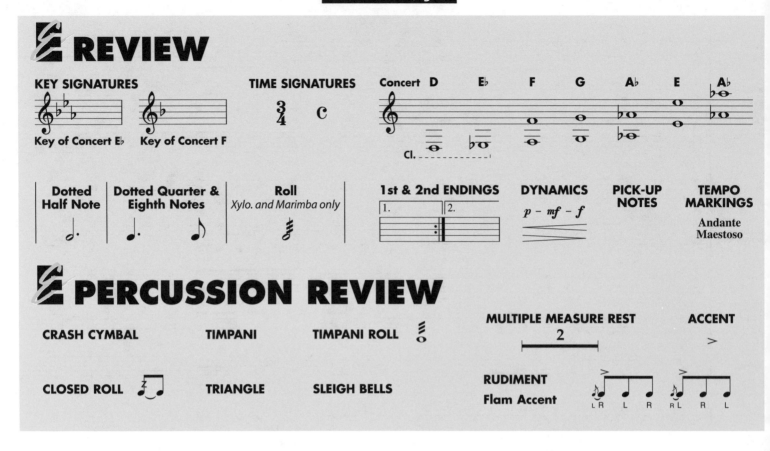

PERCUSSION REVIEW

| CRASH CYMBAL | TIMPANI | TIMPANI ROLL | MULTIPLE MEASURE REST | ACCENT |
| CLOSED ROLL | TRIANGLE | SLEIGH BELLS | RUDIMENT Flam Accent | |

TEACHING TIP This exercise includes a review of [♩. ♪], *3/4 time*, **Andante**, and the *piano dynamic marking*. Count and finger this exercise before playing.

6. AMERICA/GOD SAVE THE QUEEN

Based on a Traditional Anthem

TEACHING TIP   Review *pick-up notes* and *common time*.

7. WEARING OF THE GREEN

Irish Folk Song

TEACHING TIP   Discuss the *first and second endings.* Note the changing dynamics.

8. ROSES FROM THE SOUTH

Johann Strauss, Jr.

Student Book Page 3

TEACHING TIP   Make sure all students understand *pick-up notes* and *repeats*.

9. CRUISIN' THROUGH THE PARK

 **TEACHING TIP**   Remind players to check the key signature.
Before assigning the duet parts, play each one individually.

Oboe   Use forked fingering for all F's.

10. TRUMPET VOLUNTARY — Duet

Jeremiah Clarke

REVIEW

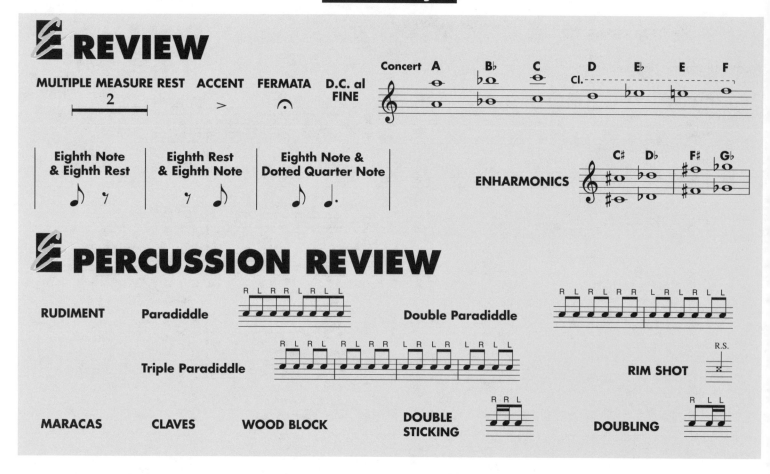

PERCUSSION REVIEW

TEACHING TIP   Reviewed in this exercise are *enharmonics, eighth rests, multiple measure rests,* and **D.C. al Fine**.

11. CHROMA-ZONE

26

TEACHING TIP   The [♪ ♩.] figure is used, creating a feel of syncopation.

Oboe   Continue using forked F fingering when moving from E♭ to D.

12. BILLY BOY

American Folk Song

TEACHING TIP Clap the rhythm of this exercise before playing emphasizing the accents and placement of the eighth rests.

13. TECHNIQUE TRAX

Roll Xylo. only

28

TEACHING TIP Play each line separately before assigning parts for a duet.
Ask students to listen for the dynamics in this exercise.

14. SALSA SIESTA – Duet

Staccato

Staccato notes are played lightly and with separation.
They are marked with a dot above or below the note.

 TEACHING TIP   Be certain that the staccato notes are played lightly.

15. TREADING LIGHTLY

Percussion
Temple Blocks   Temple Blocks (or Chinese Wood Blocks) include five different size blocks usually mounted on a stand. The hollow sounding blocks of different pitches create a distinctive and effective sound in a percussion section. For the best sound, use a soft to medium rubber mallet and play toward the edge of the top surface near the side with the open slit.

32

Tenuto

Tenuto notes are played smoothly and connected, holding each note until the next is played. They are marked with a straight line above or below the note.

 TEACHING TIP Encourage students to keep the air stream moving so that there is no separation between notes marked tenuto.

16. SMOOTH MOVE

Electric Bass

Slur A curved line which connects notes of different pitch.

Hammer on Is achieved by plucking the first note of a slurred passage with the right hand, then pressing down the second note with the left hand.

Pull off Is achieved by plucking the first note of a slurred passage with the right hand, then releasing the first note with the left hand enabling the second note to ring.

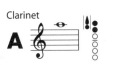

Clarinet
A

⚡ **TEACHING TIP**

On the pitch concert B♭, have students play four notes staccato and four notes legato to establish the contrast between the two styles.

Clarinet Practice long tones on all new notes.

17. SHIFTING GEARS – New Note

HISTORY

English composer **Thomas Tallis** (1508–1585) served as a royal court composer for Kings Henry VIII and Edward VI, and Queens Mary and Elizabeth. During Tallis' lifetime, the artist Michaelangelo painted the Sistine Chapel.

Canons (one or more parts imitating the first part) were used in many forms by 16th century composers. A **Round** is a strict (or exact) canon which can be repeated any number of times without stopping. Play *Tallis Canon* as a 4-part round.

TEACHING TIP Play through the canon first as one group, stressing its style and dynamics, before dividing into four parts. (Note the repeats in percussion to perform as a round.)

18. TALLIS CANON (Round)

Thomas Tallis

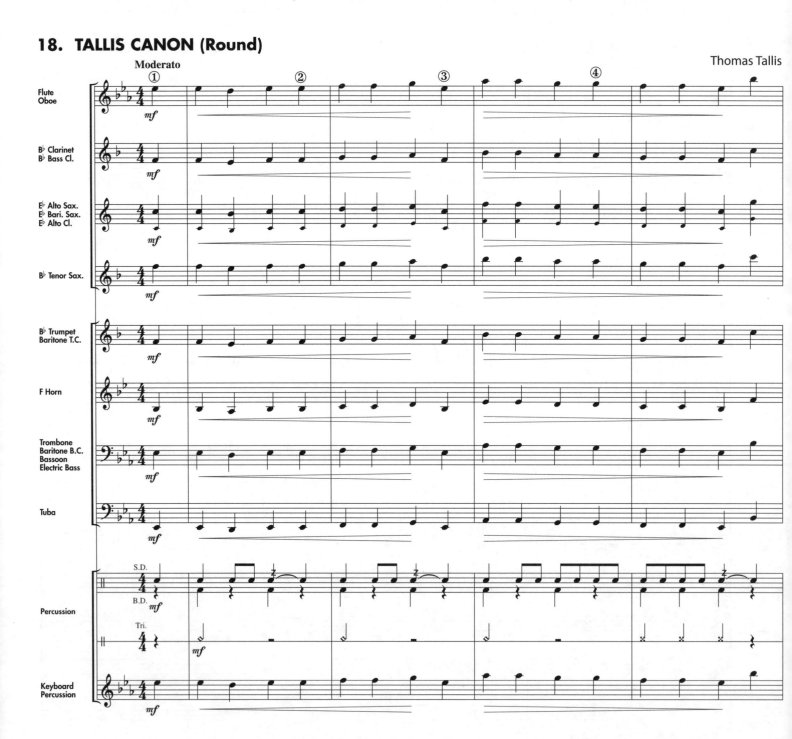

Percussion If your band does *not* perform this exercise as a round, skip the 1st ending and the repeat in your music.

Sightreading

Sightreading means playing a musical piece for the first time. The key to sightreading success is to know what to look for *before* you play. Use the word **S-T-A-R-S** to remind yourself what to look for, and eventually your band will become sightreading STARS!

S — **Sharps or flats** in the key signature
T — **Time signature** and **tempo markings**
A — **Accidentals** not found in the key signature
R — **Rhythms**, silently counting the more difficult notes and rests
S — **Signs**, including dynamics, articulations, repeats and endings

TEACHING TIP   Stress the importance of sightreading and using a logical approach (S–T–A–R–S). Consider these musical essentials you play to improve the chance for success.

19. SIGHTREADING CHALLENGE

# DAILY WARM-UPS

WORK-OUTS FOR TONE & TECHNIQUE

TEACHING TIP Exercises 20–23: These warm-up exercises are designed to help students develop tone, technique, and ensemble listening skills. They should be used daily until student book page 18.

20. TONE BUILDER

21. FLEXIBILITY STUDY

22. TECHNIQUE TRAX

Percussion   Practice Paradiddles as marked.

40

23. CHORALE

Johann Sebastian Bach

TEACHING TIP   Review staccato and tenuto articulations before playing this exercise.

24. GRANDFATHER'S CLOCK

Henry C. Work

Ritardando   *ritard.* (or) *rit.* –   Gradually slower

**TEACHING TIP**   Begin by discussing the **Allegretto** tempo marking and practicing the *rit.* in the last two measures. Stress to play together, it is necessary to watch the conductor.

25. GLOW WORM

Paul Lincke

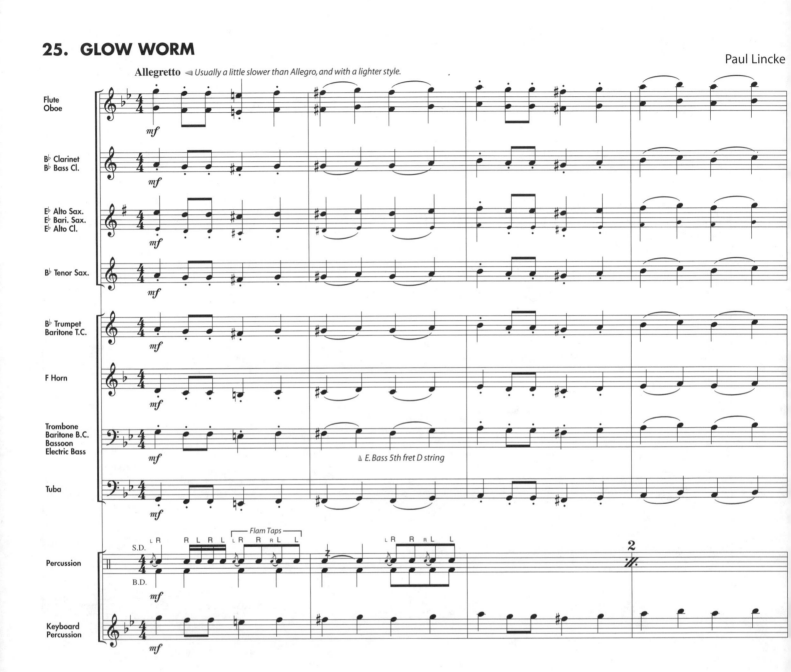

Percussion   Rudiment
Flam Paradiddle

Bass Drum Roll   Similar to a timpani roll, use two bass drum mallets of equal size and roll on the same side of the drum, playing toward opposite ends of the bass drum head for best resonance.

46

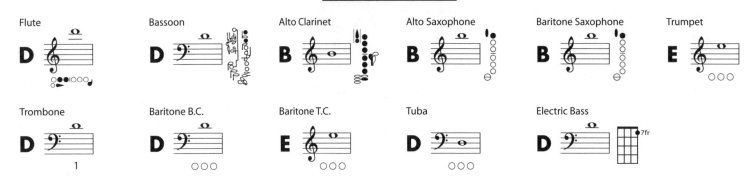

TEACHING TIP Encourage good tone quality and legato-style playing.
Emphasize watching the conductor for the release of the last note.

26. ALMA MATER – New Note *Practice long tones on all new notes.*

A.C. Weekes, W.M. Smith, H.S. Thompson

Percussion **Rudiment**
Drag   A snare drum rudiment consisting of a double bounce and a single stroke.

☰ TEACHING TIP Remind students to watch the conductor to play the *rit.* together.

27. LOCH LOMOND

Scottish Folk Song

HISTORY

Key Changes

If a key signature changes during a piece of music, you will usually see a thin double bar line at the **key change**. You may also see natural signs reminding you to "cancel" previous sharps or flats. Keep playing, using the correct notes indicated in the *new* key signature.

TEACHING TIP

Discuss the key change at the thin double bar and clap the rhythm in the second measure together before playing the exercise.

28. MOLLY MALONE

Irish Folk Song

Dynamics

cresc. = crescendo (or)
decresc. = decrescendo (or)

TEACHING TIP Prepare for this exercise by practicing *cresc.* and *decresc.* on a single pitch.

29. RISE AND FALL

TEACHING TIP   Before playing this exercise, review its articulations.

30. NO COMPARISON

TEACHING TIP   Use the S–T–A–R–S acronym to help students improve sightreading skills.

31. SIGHTREADING CHALLENGE   *Remember the S-T-A-R-S guidelines.*

 **Time Signature**
Cut Time (Alla Breve)

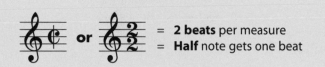

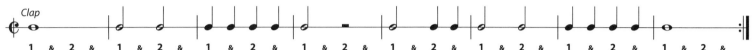

TEACHING TIP Discuss the note values in cut time. Then, have students clap and count two measures at a time before trying the entire exercise.

32. RHYTHM RAP   *Clap the rhythm while counting and tapping.*

TEACHING TIP Have students count this exercise while performing the fingerings before playing.

33. A CUT ABOVE

TEACHING TIP   Make sure that everyone understands the 2/4 time signature, then count and finger this exercise before playing.

34. TWO-FOUR YANKEE DOODLE

American Folk Song

TEACHING TIP   Review the cut time signature.

35. CUT TIME YANKEE DOODLE

American Folk Song

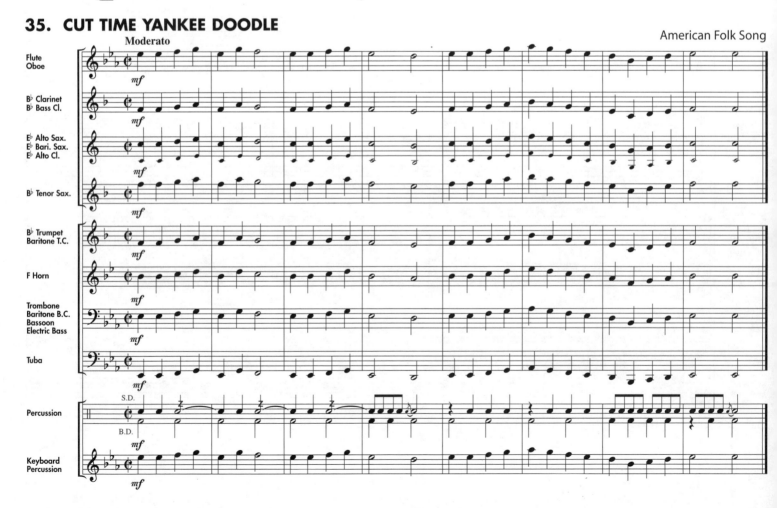

TEACHING TIP Have students count and finger this exercise before playing.

36. MARIANNE

Jamaican Folk Song

54

⚡ **TEACHING TIP** Discuss the dotted half note in cut time; have students write in the counting for the entire exercise.

Percussion Review Right Hand Lead sticking pattern.

37. THE VICTORS

Louis Elbel

Rolls Xylo. only

⚡ **TEACHING TIP**   Encourage students to write in the counting for extra credit.

38. ESSENTIAL CREATIVITY *Write this example in cut time* **¢** *before playing.*

Dynamics

mp — *mezzo piano* (moderately soft)

Use full breath support at all dynamic levels.

p — mp — mf — f

Percussion Dynamics

p — *piano* (softly): *bring sticks close to head*

mp — *mezzo piano* (moderately soft): *lift sticks a little higher*

mf — *mezzo forte* (moderately loud): *normal stick height*

f — *forte* (loudly): *lift sticks even higher*

Tenor Saxophone

D **TEACHING TIP** Observing the dynamics, students should count and clap this exercise before playing.

39. A - ROVING – New Note

Syncopation

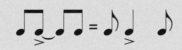

Syncopation occurs when an accent or emphasis is given to a note that is not on a strong beat. This type of "off-beat" feel is common in many popular and classical styles.

THEORY

TEACHING TIP Discuss the syncopation definition that is highlighted in the student book. As the students count and clap this exercise, be certain that they emphasize the accents.

40. RHYTHM RAP

⚡ **TEACHING TIP**   Before playing, have students emphasize the syncopated notes as they count and finger this exercise.

41. IN SYNC

⚡ **TEACHING TIP**   Point out the syncopated notes before playing this exercise.

Percussion   Optional: The Sus. Cym. and Snare Drum parts can be played by one person if desired.

42. LA ROCA

Puerto Rican Folk Song

(Ex. 43)
American composer **George M. Cohan** (1878–1942) was also a popular author, producer, director and performer. He helped develop a popular form of American musical theater now known as musical comedy. He is also considered to be one of the most famous composers of American patriotic songs, earning the Congressional Medal of Honor in 1917 for his song *Over There*. Many of his songs became morale boosters when the United States entered World War I in that same year.

HISTORY

TEACHING TIP   Quiz Assessment – Pick-up notes, accents, syncopation, dynamics, and accidentals.

43. ESSENTIAL ELEMENTS QUIZ – YOU'RE A GRAND OLD FLAG

George M. Cohan

New Key Signature

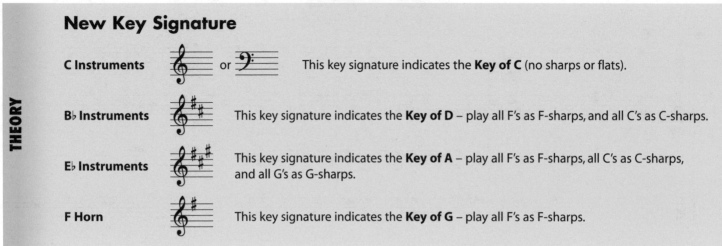

C Instruments — This key signature indicates the **Key of C** (no sharps or flats).

B♭ Instruments — This key signature indicates the **Key of D** – play all F's as F-sharps, and all C's as C-sharps.

E♭ Instruments — This key signature indicates the **Key of A** – play all F's as F-sharps, all C's as C-sharps, and all G's as G-sharps.

F Horn — This key signature indicates the **Key of G** – play all F's as F-sharps.

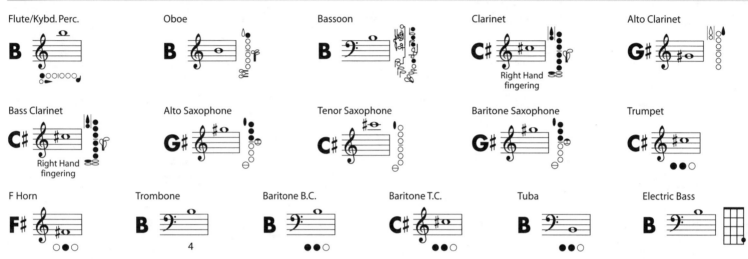

TEACHING TIP — Discuss the new key signature. Practice the new note and make sure the clarinets understand the right hand C♯.

44. KEY MOMENT – New Note

Percussion This exercise can be used as a daily warm-up to develop forearm muscles.

 **TEACHING TIP**   Remind students about the key signature. Also, stress that notes before breath marks should still be given full value.

45. THE MINSTREL BOY

Irish Folk Song

64

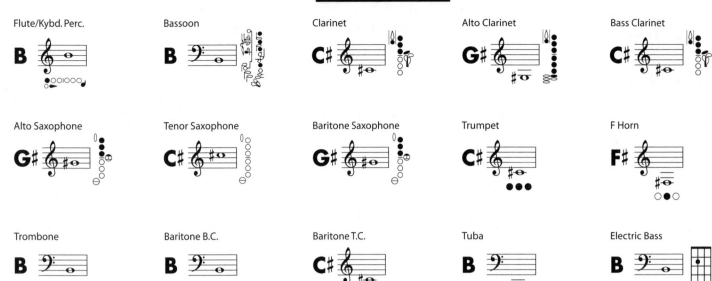

TEACHING TIP   Play the new note before playing this exercise and review staccato.

46. CLOSE CALL – New Note

THEORY

Cut Time Syncopation

$\frac{2}{4}$ ♪ ♩   ♪ = ¢ ♩ ♩   ♩

Compare the notation of the melody below with *Victory March*. Should they sound the same?

TEACHING TIP   Review cut time and then have the students write in the counting. Ask whether exercise 47 and 48 should sound the same.

48. WINNING STREAK

M. J. Shea

68

TEACHING TIP Ask the students what each letter of the S–T–A–R–S acronym means and have them review it with respect to this exercise.

49. SIGHTREADING CHALLENGE *Remember the S-T-A-R-S guidelines.*

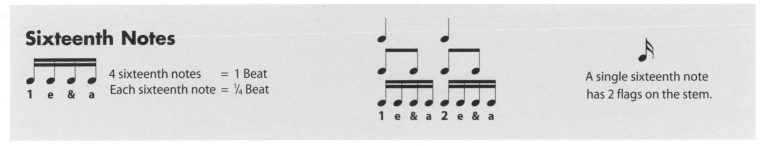

Sixteenth Notes

1 e & a

4 sixteenth notes = 1 Beat
Each sixteenth note = ¼ Beat

1 e & a 2 e & a

A single sixteenth note has 2 flags on the stem.

TEACHING TIP Introduce sixteenth notes and practice their counting (1–e–&–a). Clap and count each measure of this exercise one at a time.

50. RHYTHM RAP

51. SIXTEENTH NOTE FANFARE

TEACHING TIP Count and finger this exercise before playing. Make sure the tempo remains steady.

TEACHING TIP   Count and finger this exercise first, maintaining a steady beat.

52. MOVING ALONG

(Ex. 53)
Percussion

Tom-Tom   Composers use this term to describe a wide variety of drums without snares. Common instruments include the double headed tom-toms on drum set, and the single headed concert tom-toms mounted on stands. Use sticks or felt mallets on the tom-tom. A snare drum with snares off may be used as a substitute.

TEACHING TIP   Prepare by having half of the students clap and count line A while the other half clap and count line B.

53. BACK AND FORTH – Duet

72

Oboe

C

 **TEACHING TIP**   Play at a slow, steady tempo before moving up to **Moderato**.
Point out the syncopation in measure 5.

54. COMIN' ROUND THE MOUNTAIN VARIATIONS – New Note

American Folk Song

▲   ▲

Percussion

Drum Set   The practice of one person playing several drums and cymbals in a sitting position began with the "trap drummers" in the late 1890's and early 1900's in travelling shows, the circus, and the theatre pit. Today, drum set has become an important part of many styles of music groups including jazz ensembles, rock 'n' roll bands, and pit orchestras.

To learn the basics, start with the three primary sounds of a drum set:

Suspended Cymbal – usually called "Ride Cymbal" and played with the right hand.

Snare Drum – played with the left hand.

Bass Drum – played with a foot pedal.

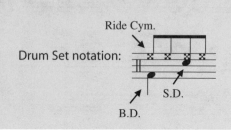

Ride Cym.

Drum Set notation:

S.D.

B.D.

74

TEACHING TIP   Quiz assessment – Sixteenth notes, accents, syncopation, and counting rests.

55. ESSENTIAL ELEMENTS QUIZ

Percussion Use Flam Paradiddle Sticking when playing the 16th note groups.

PERFORMANCE SPOTLIGHT

 **TEACHING TIP** Exercises 56–62 can be used as a cumulative review of previous material and/or as a prepared band concert. Other items which could be added to the concert include demonstrations of the various instrument families and highlights from earlier material.

56. WARM-UP CHORALE

J. S. Bach/Arr. by John Higgins

76

57. THE THUNDERER – Band Arrangement

John Philip Sousa
Arr. by John Higgins

Percussion

Bongos

Bongos are the highest pitched hand drums in the Latin American percussion family. Traditionally, bongos with skin heads are played with the fingers while sitting down, holding the bongos between the knees with the larger drum on the right. Bongos are also available with plastic heads mounted on a stand. These bongos can be played with thin sticks or small, hard felt mallets.

58. HILL AND GULLY RIDER – Band Arrangement

Jamaican Folk Song
Arr. by John Higgins

7
11
Flute
Oboe
B♭ Clarinet
E♭ Alto Sax.
B♭ Tenor Sax.
B♭ Trumpet
F Horn
Low Brass &
Woodwinds
Percussion
Keyboard
Percussion
mf
f
p
2
1.
2.
a2

59. SHENANDOAH – Band Arrangement

American Folk Song
Arr. by John Higgins

(Ex. 60)
Percussion

Guiro   The guiro (pronounced *we'ro*) is a Latin American instrument usually in the shape of a gourd with hollowed-out notches on the side. It is played by scraping a stick along the notched side. A good sound will result if you keep constant pressure on the stick while scraping.

Cross Stick Rim Shot   Place the tip of the left stick in the middle of the head and gently strike the left stick with the right just in front of where you are holding the stick.

PERFORMANCE SPOTLIGHT

60. LAS MAÑANITAS – Band Arrangement

Mexican Folk Song
Arr. by John Higgins

61. RONDEAU – Band Arrangement

Jean-Joseph Mouret
Arr. by John Higgins

March Style (♩ = ca. 108)

D.S. al Fine—Go back to the sign (𝄋) and play until **Fine**.

62. ROCK.COM – Encore Band Arrangement

John Higgins

88

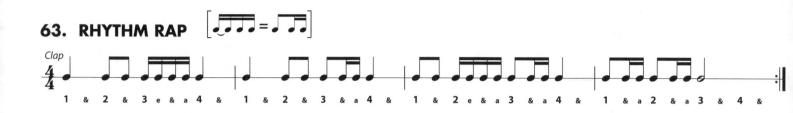

TEACHING TIP   Clap and count measure two as a preparatory exercise.

63. RHYTHM RAP

TEACHING TIP   Count and finger this exercise in a steady rhythm before playing.

64. SIXTEENTH VARIATIONS

Percussion

Tambourine Knee to Fist Technique

The preferred method for playing rapid passages is the knee to fist technique. Position your foot on a small stool so that the knee is raised. Hold the tambourine above your knee with the head facing down and close your other hand over the open end of the tambourine to form a fist. Move the tambourine to the knee (it should bounce off of the top of the knee), then up to the closed fist, following the K and F markings in the music.

TEACHING TIP   Count and finger this exercise before playing. Students should count in a staccato style when it occurs and also observe dynamics (note the *cresc.*).

65. SEA CHANTEY

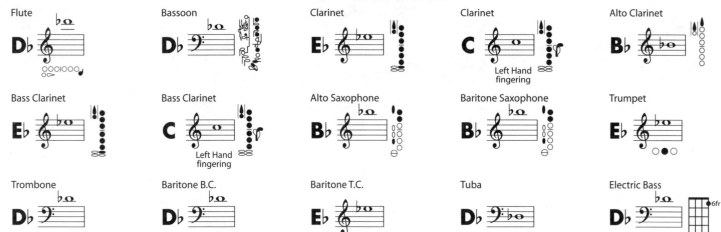

TEACHING TIP Practice the new note before playing this exercise.

66. AMERICAN FANFARE – New Note

New Key Signature (Ex. 67)

C Instruments 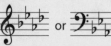 This key signature indicates the **Key of Ab** – play all B's as B-flats, all E's as E-flats, all A's as A-flats, and all D's as D-flats.

Bb Instruments This key signature indicates the **Key of Bb** – play all B's as B-flats, and all E's as E-flats.

Eb Instruments This key signature indicates the **Key of F** – play all B's as B-flats.

F Horn This key signature indicates the **Key of Eb** – play all B's as B-flats, all E's as E-flats, and all A's as A-flats.

THEORY

Clarinet
B♭

Electric Bass   A♭ Major Scale Fingering.   5fr   Try A♭ major scale fingering.

🏴 **TEACHING TIP**   Explain the new key signature before beginning this exercise.
Encourage students to use faster air as they play up the scale.

67. SCALE STUDY – New Note

▲

Percussion Flam Rudiment Review

This exercise includes Flam Taps (measures 1–2), Flam Paradiddles (measures 3–4), and Flams (measures 4 and 7). Observe all stickings carefully.

 **TEACHING TIP**   Make sure the clarinets understand their left hand C fingering and have them practice the interval C to E♭ (in the staff) before playing this exercise.

68. BILL BAILEY

Hughie Cannon

Percussion
Crash Cymbal Chokes
(Hi-Hat Style)

Hold the cymbals in a horizontal position with the edges of the cymbals closed against your stomach and open facing away from you. Using the edges close to your stomach as a hinge, close the cymbals on the beats, and open them on the rests.

94

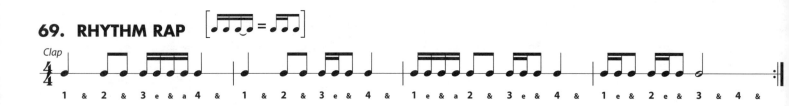

TEACHING TIP First, clap and count [♪♫ ♩]. Then, clap and count one measure at a time before playing the entire exercise.

69. RHYTHM RAP

TEACHING TIP Count and finger this exercise in a steady rhythm before playing.

70. RHYTHM ETUDE

TEACHING TIP Make sure the students observe the dynamics as they first count and finger this exercise.

71. BATTLE STATIONS

TEACHING TIP   Have the students circle the dynamic markings. Before playing, review the [♪♫] figure.

Electric Bass Try using only 3rd fret through 6th fret positions.

72. ENGLISH DANCE

🎵 **TEACHING TIP** Review the [♪♫] and [♫♪] rhythmic figures. Make sure the dynamics and accents are observed.

73. BIG ROCK CANDY MOUNTAIN

American Folk Song

Percussion **Tambourine Sixteenth Note Technique**

Hold the tambourine in a vertical position. To play four sixteenth notes, move the tambourine toward the opposite hand, then back, then move the tambourine to the heel of the opposite hand (for the accent), then back. Repeat for each group of sixteenth notes.

98

TEACHING TIP Quiz assessment – Key, [♫♩], [♫♩], dynamics, slurs, and **D.C. al Fine**.

Electric Bass Use A♭ major scale fingering.

74. ESSENTIAL ELEMENTS QUIZ

Rallentando   *rall.* – Gradually slower (same as ritardando)

TEACHING TIP   First, conduct the last two measures while the students clap and count them, following the conductor carefully.

75. SIMPLE SONG – Duet

 **TEACHING TIP** As a preparatory exercise, play the first two measures, stressing the different articulations.

Percussion Review the Flamcue Rudiment.

76. LINE DANCE

🎵 **TEACHING TIP** Count and finger this exercise, keeping a steady rhythm.
Then, play it, emphasizing steady, even sixteenth notes.

77. TECHNIQUE TRAX

TEACHING TIP   To avoid rushing or uneven sixteenth notes, have the students first count and finger the exercise, then tongue the exercise (omit the slurs), and finally play it as written.

78. THE GALWAY PIPER

Irish Reel

TEACHING TIP Have students write the counting under the notes.

79. MANHATTAN BEACH MARCH

John Philip Sousa

Student Book Page 16

**TEACHING TIP**   Review the S–T–A–R–S acronym and then have the students play the exercise.
Encourage the proper performance of articulations as a part of sightreading success.

80. SIGHTREADING CHALLENGE   *Remember the S-T-A-R-S guidelines.*

81. RHYTHM RAP

82. MARCHING ALONG

TEACHING TIP To properly balance the chords with a full ensemble, have the low brass and woodwinds play part C.

83. FANFARE FOR BAND – Trio

TEACHING TIP Review the dotted rhythms.

84. O TANNENBAUM

German Carol

📐 **TEACHING TIP** Have half the class count and finger this exercise while the other half plays it, observing the articulations. Strive for a steady tempo throughout.

Electric Bass Use A♭ major scale fingering.

85. S'VIVON

Traditional Hanukkah Song

Student Book Page 17

TEACHING TIP Point out where the repeat occurs. Encourage playing the staccato notes lightly and giving the tenuto notes full value.

86. GOOD KING WENCESLAS

English Carol

110

WORK-OUTS FOR TONE & TECHNIQUE

 Exercise 87–90: Students should now begin to use these new daily warm-ups to help continue their development of tone, technique, and ensemble listening skills.

Percussion
Double Bounce A double bounce is a controlled multiple bounce consisting of only two bounces per stroke. Rolls that use double bounces are called **open** (measured) rolls.

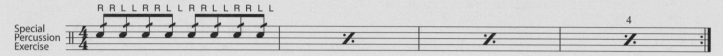

Percussion This exercise shows the correct number of hand motions and strokes for the **Five Stroke Roll** (measures 2–4) and the **Nine Stroke Roll** (measure 5). Use the Double Bounce Technique of one hand motion for two strokes (bounces).

87. TONE BUILDER *Play at a very slow tempo.*

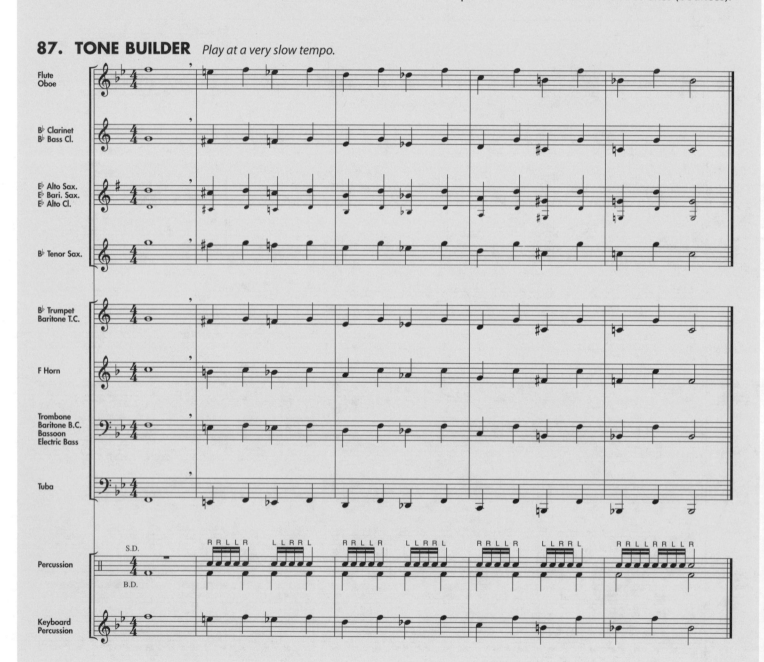

Clarinet, Bass Clarinet Try "Right Hand B" for smoother technique.
Percussion This example shows how open five stroke rolls are written in music.
Use the same technique from the previous exercise for these rolls.

88. FLEXIBILITY STUDY

Electric Bass Use A♭ major scale fingering.
Percussion This example shows how open nine stroke rolls are written in music. Use the same technique from Ex. 87 for these rolls.

89. TECHNIQUE TRAX

90. CHORALE

Johann Sebastian Bach

TEACHING TIP Stress the importance of properly playing the articulations and the [♪ ♪] rhythm for a good musical performance.

91. TOREADOR SONG (from CARMEN)

Georges Bizet

French composer **Georges Bizet** (1838–1875) entered the Paris Conservatory to study music when he was only ten years old. There he won many awards for voice, piano, organ, and composition. Bizet's best known composition is the opera *Carmen*, which was first performed in 1875. *Carmen* tells the story of a band of Gypsies, soldiers, smugglers, and outlaws. Originally criticized for its realism on stage, it was soon hailed as the most popular French opera ever written.

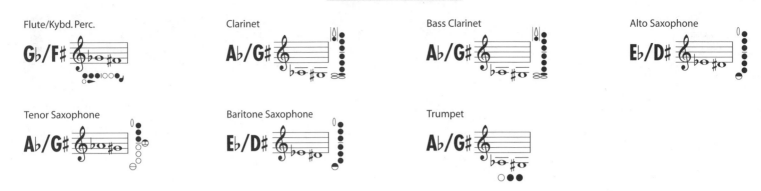

TEACHING TIP   Play the new notes and review enharmonics.

Percussion   Use the same hand motions from the previous five stroke rolls for the five stroke rolls used here in measures 1, 3, and 5.

92. LA CUMPARSITA – New Note (Enharmonic)

G. Rodriguez

Percussion
Timbales   Timbales are the middle range drums of Latin American percussion instruments. These single headed drums have shallow metal shells and are mounted on a stand. Use thin sticks to play the timbales, striking the head about one third of the way from the edge of the head.

118

TEACHING TIP   Review syncopation and ask students to identify where it occurs.

Electric Bass   Use A♭ major scale fingering.

93. THE YELLOW ROSE OF TEXAS *Check the key signature.*

American Folk Song

120

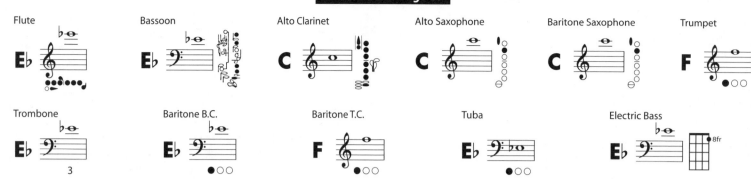

TEACHING TIP   Try playing this exercise slowly at first, gradually increasing the tempo.

Electric Bass   Eb Major Scale Fingering.   Try Eb major scale fingering.

Percussion   Use the same hand motions from the previous nine stroke rolls for the nine stroke rolls used here in measures 1, 3, 4, and 8.

94. SCALE STUDY – New Note

**TEACHING TIP** Before playing the entire exercise, practice the last four measures with the pick-up, discussing *rit., a tempo*, and having everyone watch the conductor.

95. ADVANCE AUSTRALIA FAIR

Peter Dodds McCormick

Until 1974 Australia's official national anthem was *God Save The Queen*. A competition was held in 1973 to compose a new anthem, but none of the entries met with the judges' approval. Finally the government asked the public to vote, choosing from among Australia's 3 most popular patriotic songs. After easily defeating *Waltzing Matilda* and *God Save The Queen, Advance Australia Fair* was officially declared the national anthem of Australia on April 19, 1974.

TEACHING TIP   Ask volunteers to play their completed lines for the class.

96. ESSENTIAL CREATIVITY

Arrange the melody of "America (My Country 'Tis Of Thee)" for your instrument. Write out the first line (6 measures).
Your first note is Concert F. ADD: Key signature—key of Concert F • Time signature—3/4 • Tempo and dynamic markings.

Play the completed line on your instrument to hear your own version.

TEACHING TIP Have half the students count and finger this exercise while the other half plays. Then, switch before having everyone play together.

97. AMERICAN PATROL

F. W. Meacham

 **TEACHING TIP** Stress playing the [♩.♪] rhythm accurately.

98. ARIA (from MARRIAGE OF FIGARO)

Wolfgang Amadeus Mozart

(music score — Flute/Oboe, Bb Clarinet/Bb Bass Cl., Eb Alto Sax./Eb Bari. Sax./Eb Alto Cl., Bb Tenor Sax., Bb Trumpet/Baritone T.C., F Horn, Trombone/Baritone B.C./Bassoon/Electric Bass, Tuba, Percussion, Keyboard Percussion)

(Ex. 99)
American composer **John Philip Sousa** (1854–1932) was best known for his brilliant band marches.
Sousa wrote 136 marches, including *The Stars and Stripes Forever,* which was declared the official march
of the United States of America in 1987.

HISTORY

New Notes for Ex. 99

Clarinet

Right Hand

Bass Clarinet

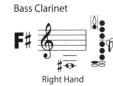

Right Hand

TEACHING TIP   Be sure all students understand the [♩. ♪] rhythm in cut time.

99. THE STARS AND STRIPES FOREVER   Percussion   John Philip Sousa

Student Book Page 20

TEACHING TIP   Before playing, review the S–T–A–R–S acronym.

Electric Bass   Use A♭ major scale fingering.

100. SIGHTREADING CHALLENGE   *Remember the S-T-A-R-S guidelines.*

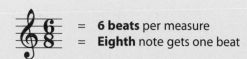

6/8 Time Signature

	= **6 beats** per measure	♪ = 1 beat	♩ = 2 beats
	= **Eighth** note gets one beat	♩. = 3 beats	♩.. = 6 beats

6/8 time is usually played with a slight emphasis on the **1st** and **4th** beats of each measure. This divides the measure into 2 groups of 3 beats each. In faster music, these two primary beats will make the music feel like it's counted "in 2."

TEACHING TIP   Carefully explain the 6/8 time signature. Then, clap and count each measure separately, making certain that everyone understands the note values.

101. RHYTHM RAP   *Clap the rhythm while counting and tapping.*

TEACHING TIP   This rhythm matches that of exercise 101.

102. LAZY DAY

132

TEACHING TIP   Have the students write in the rhythms before playing.

103. ROW YOUR BOAT

Percussion

Multiple Bounce in $\frac{6}{8}$ Time Signature

Use the sticking pattern from the eighth note pulse and connect with multiple bounces to sound as smooth as possible.

🎼 **TEACHING TIP** Make sure everyone understands the pick-up note, then count and finger the exercise before playing.

104. JOLLY GOOD FELLOW

🎼 **TEACHING TIP** Have half the class play while the other half counts and fingers this exercise. Then, switch before having everyone play together.

105. CHANSON

French Folk Song

134

TEACHING TIP Quiz assessment – 6/8 time, rhythms, and dynamics. Make sure that the [♩ ♪] rhythms are not played like [♩♪] rhythms.

Bs. Cl. Try "right Hand E" for smoother technique.

106. ESSENTIAL ELEMENTS QUIZ – WHEN JOHNNY COMES MARCHING HOME

American Folk Song

Flute
Oboe
B♭ Clarinet
B♭ Bass Cl.
E♭ Alto Sax.
E♭ Bari. Sax.
E♭ Alto Cl.
B♭ Tenor Sax.
B♭ Trumpet
Baritone T.C.
F Horn
Trombone
Baritone B.C.
Bassoon
Electric Bass
Tuba
Percussion
Keyboard
Percussion
cresc.
f
R

136

THEORY

More Enharmonics

Remember that notes which sound the same but have different letter names are called **enharmonics**. These are some common enharmonics that you'll use in the exercises below.

More Chromatics

The smallest distance between two notes is a half-step, and a scale made up of consecutive half-steps is a **chromatic scale.** These are usually written with **enharmonic** notes—sharps when going up and flats when going down.

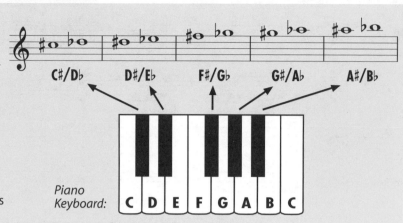

Piano Keyboard:

Clarinet
F#/Gb
Chromatic fingering

Bass Clarinet
F#/Gb
Chromatic fingering

Tenor Saxophone
F#/Gb
Alternate fingering

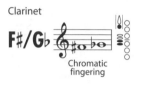

TEACHING TIP   Clarinets and saxophones should practice the appropriate alternate fingerings before playing this chromatic scale.

Winds   Practice slowly until you are sure of all the fingerings/positions.

Percussion   The sixteenth notes preceding the 17 stroke rolls use the same number of hand motions. The hand motions never change speed; just go from single strokes to double bounces (open rolls).

Kybd. Perc.   Practice slowly until you are sure of all the notes.

107. CHROMATIC SCALE

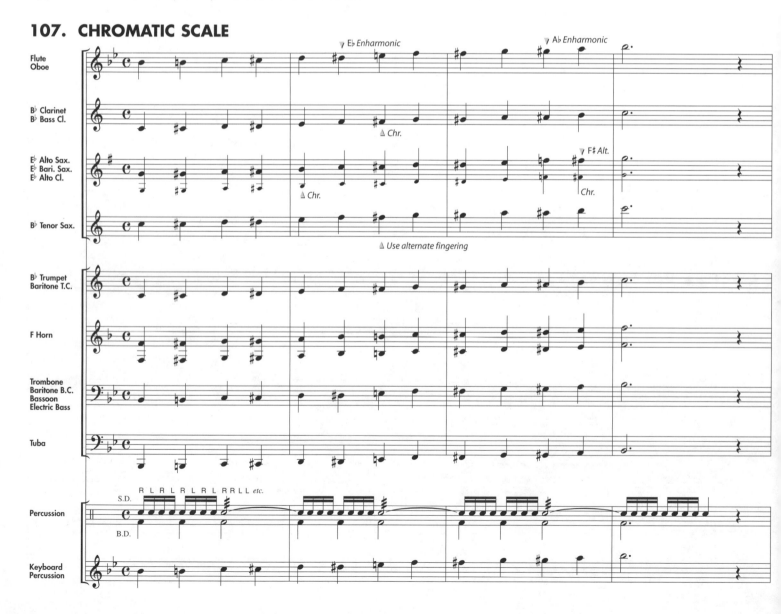

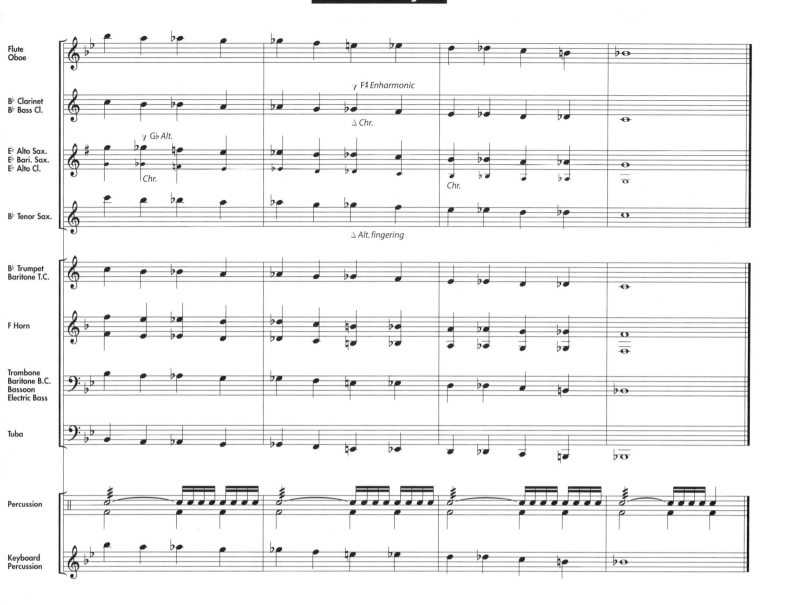

138

TEACHING TIP Practice slowly at first and gradually increase the tempo.

Kybd. Perc. Practice with the following sticking patterns: **A.** R L R L R **B.** L R L R L **C.** R R L L R **D.** L L R R L

108. TECHNIQUE TRAX

(Ex. 99)
A **Habañera** is a Cuban dance and song form in slow 2/4 meter. It is named after the city of Havana, the capital of Cuba. Made popular in the New World in the early 19th Century, it was later carried over to Spain. There the rhythms of the Habañera were incorporated into many styles of Latin music. One of the most famous Habañeras is heard in Bizet's *Carmen*, written in 1875.

HISTORY

Clarinet   C#/Db   Left Hand fingering
Bass Clarinet   C#/Db   Left Hand fingering

TEACHING TIP Review the correct fingerings before playing this exercise.

109. HABAÑERA (from CARMEN)

Georges Bizet

Percussion

Tambourine Thumb Roll

In addition to the tambourine shake, another method of producing a sustained sound on the tambourine is the thumb roll. Holding the tambourine in the left hand, begin by placing the right thumb at 3 o'clock on the head. Move the thumb slowly with slight pressure in a counter-clockwise direction toward 9 o'clock. The proper combination of thumb pressure and slow speed will produce a sustained sound on the tambourine.

TEACHING TIP Review the chromatic and alternate fingerings. Make sure that the tempo does not increase as the students play the *cresc.*

110. CHROMATIC CRESCENDO

TEACHING TIP   Remind students not to rush the four slurred sixteenth notes and to tongue beat two in measures 3 and 7.

111. TURKISH MARCH (from THE RUINS OF ATHENS)

Ludwig van Beethoven

TEACHING TIP   Be sure notes preceding breath marks are given their full value.

112. THE OVERLANDER

Australian Folk Song

TEACHING TIP Point out the key change at the end of the first line. Note the enharmonics and check for correct alternate fingerings.

Percussion Review the double sticking patterns used in this example. Can you identify the rudiment in measure 4?
Review the knee to fist technique on page 14-A.

113. STACCATO STUDY

144

TEACHING TIP   Ask students where the syncopated notes occur.

114. YANKEE DOODLE DANDY

George M. Cohan

TEACHING TIP Ask students to identify the number of counts each note receives in this exercise.
Review S–T–A–R–S and have students play the exercise.

 **115. SIGHTREADING CHALLENGE**
Remember the **S–T–A–R–S** guidelines:
S – Sharps or flats in the key signature, **T** – Time signature and tempos, **A** – Accidentals, **R** – Rhythm, **S** – Signs

Triplets

A **triplet** is a group of **3** notes played in the space of **2**. In 2/4, 3/4, or 4/4 time , an eighth note triplet is spread evenly across one beat.

THEORY

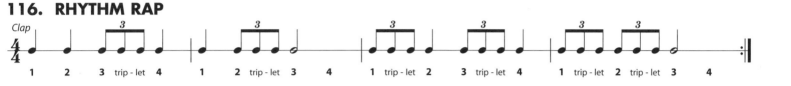

🎼 **TEACHING TIP**   Explain the triplets. Then, clap and count each measure separately before trying the entire exercise.

116. RHYTHM RAP

🎼 **TEACHING TIP**   The rhythm from exercise 116 appears here as well.

117. THREE TO GET READY

TEACHING TIP Have half the students play while the others count and finger this exercise.
Then, switch before having everyone play together.

118. TRIPLET STUDY

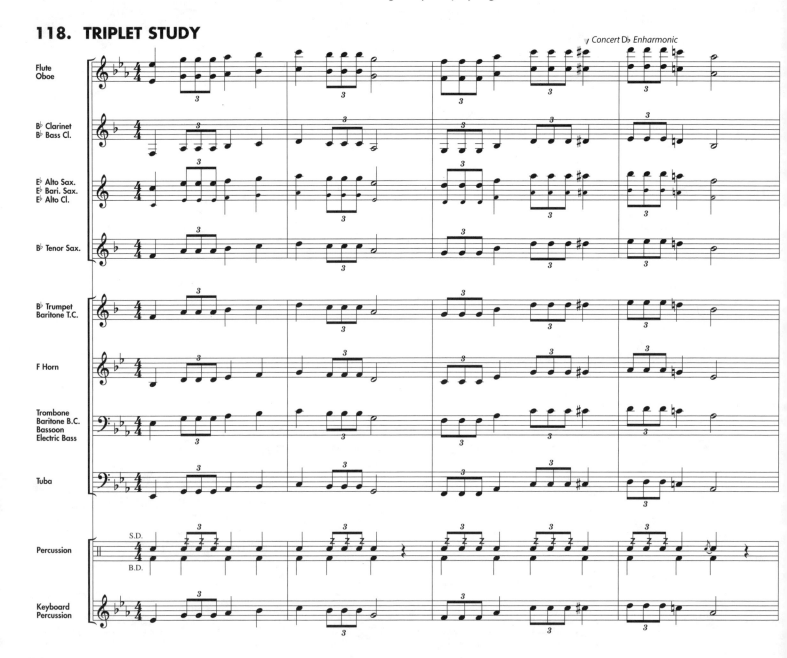

150

TEACHING TIP   Have the low brass and woodwinds play line B.

119. MARCH (from THE NUTCRACKER) – Duet

Peter I. Tchaikovsky

152

⧨ **TEACHING TIP**   Quiz assessment – Key, accents, staccato, and triplets.

120. ESSENTIAL ELEMENTS QUIZ – THEME FROM FAUST

Charles Gounod

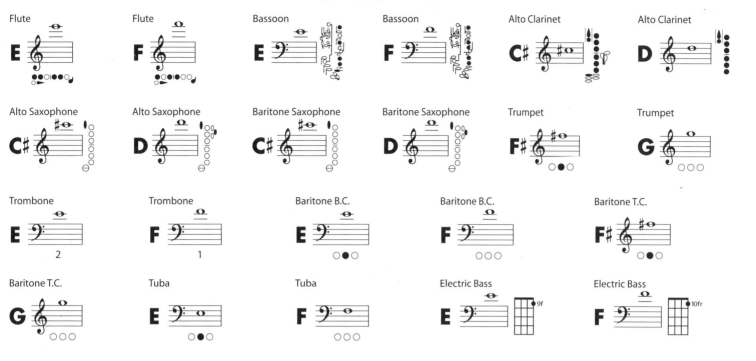

TEACHING TIP Remind students to give the quarter note before the quarter rest its full value.
If the triplets are not being played evenly, have the students clap and count them.

Flute Move your jaw and bottom lip forward as the scale ascends.

Electric Bass F Major Scale Fingering. Try F major scale fingering.

121. SCALE STUDY New Note

TEACHING TIP   Have students write in the counting before playing this exercise.

Electric Bass   Try F major scale fingering.

122. OVER THE RIVER AND THROUGH THE WOODS

American Folk Song

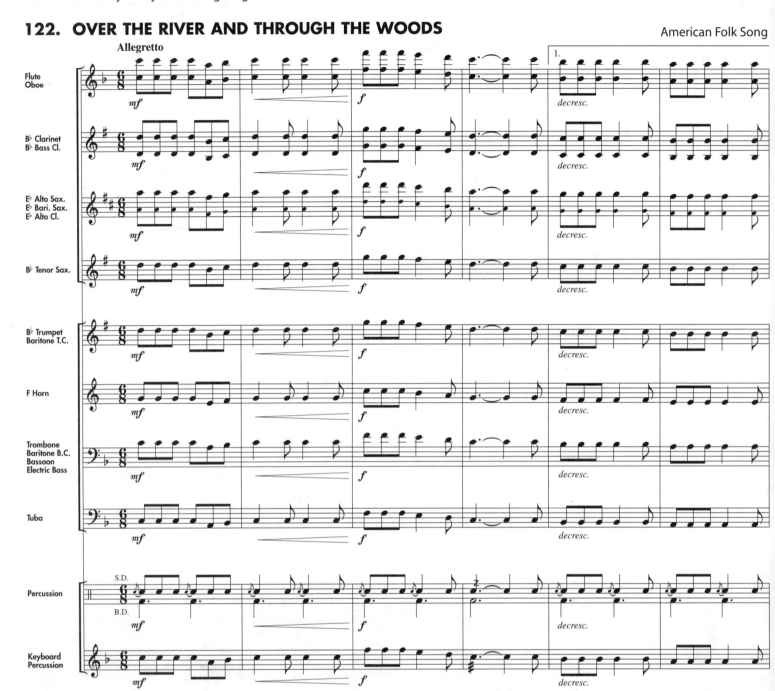

156

TEACHING TIP   To prepare, count and clap measures 3 and 4.

123. RHYTHM RAP

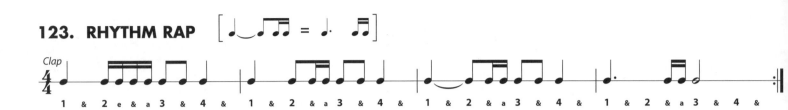

TEACHING TIP   The rhythm here matches that of exercise 123.

124. ON THE MOVE

Percussion

Hi-Hat   The hi-hat was introduced in the 1920's and is now a standard piece of equipment for the drum set. A small pair of cymbals are mounted on a stand, and a foot pedal allows the top cymbal to open and close on the bottom cymbal. The hi-hat is played with sticks with the cymbals in either a closed position or alternating between open and closed positions.

TEACHING TIP Play the first measure by itself, observing the articulations before playing the entire exercise. Stress a steady tempo.

125. HIGHER GROUND

TEACHING TIP   Quiz assessment – Sixteenth notes, dotted quarter notes, and dynamics.

126. ESSENTIAL ELEMENTS QUIZ

HISTORY

The first known printing of the lyrics and music to **The Marines' Hymn** dates from August 1, 1918. An unknown author is believed to have taken the opening words of the song from the words on the Marine Corps flag, "From the halls of Montezuma to the shores of Tripoli." The music was taken from "Genevieve de Brabant," by the operetta composer Jacques Offenbach.

TEACHING TIP   Have students first clap and count the first eight measures with the pick-up.

Percussion

127. THE MARINES' HYMN

162

D.S. al Fine

Play until you see the **D.S. al Fine**. Then so back to the sign (𝄋) and play until the word **Fine**. **D.S.** is the abbreviation for **Dal Segno**, or "from the sign," and **Fine** means "the end."

TEACHING TIP   Ask a volunteer to explain the difference between **D.C. al Fine** and **D.S. al Fine**.

128. D.S. MARCH

164

Accelerando

accel. – Gradually faster.

TEACHING TIP Practice the *accel.* by following the conductor on repeated quarter notes.

129. CAN–CAN

Jacques Offenbach

⚡ **TEACHING TIP**   Write in the counting before playing this exercise.

130. TARANTELLA

Italian Folk Song

Percussion
Natural Sticking

In order to obtain the proper feel when playing music in 6/8, percussionists often use natural sticking to enhance the phrasing. By applying an alternate sticking of R L R L R L to each measure, then remove the sticking when there is a rest, you are left with the natural sticking for the piece.

THEORY

The **waltz** is a dance in moderate 3/4 time which developed around 1800 from the Ländler, an Austrian peasant dance. Austrian composer **Johann Strauss, Jr.** (1825–1899) composed over 400 waltzes. These include such famous pieces as *The Blue Danube, Tales From the Vienna Woods* and *Emperor Waltz*.

TEACHING TIP   Have a student explain the first and second endings.

131. EMPEROR WALTZ

Johann Strauss, Jr.

Legato Style

legato – Played in a smooth, connected style.

TEACHING TIP Play each line separately before assigning parts.

Percussion Use natural sticking.

132. ENGLISH DANCE – Duet

Johann Christian Bach

170

 **TEACHING TIP**   Quiz assessment – Key, pick-up note, [♩ ♪], first and second ending repeat, slurs, and dynamics.

133. ESSENTIAL ELEMENTS QUIZ – BRITISH GRENADIERS

Traditional

(Ex. 134)
Percussion

Congas Congas are the largest hand drums in the Latin American percussion family. Traditionally, they are played as a single drum from a sitting position, but a double set of drums on a stand is also quite popular. While the Bongos use more of a finger technique, the Congas use the entire hand on the skin to produce the fullest sound. The printed hand motions will allow you to avoid crossing hands when you play.

172

🎓 **TEACHING TIP**   Ask students where the syncopated notes occur.

134. NASSAU BOUND

Bahamian Folk Song

174

TEACHING TIP   Observe the accidentals and listen for legato playing.

135. UNFINISHED SYMPHONY THEME

Franz Schubert

TEACHING TIP Clap and count this exercise before playing.

Percussion Review flams, flam taps, and drags.

136. RHYTHM STUDY

Measure Repeat ⁒ Repeat the previous measure once for each **Measure Repeat** sign.

 **TEACHING TIP** Show the students the measure repeat sign and explain how it is used.
Then, play measures 5 and 6 before beginning the exercise.

137. COUNTRY GARDENS

English Folk Song

🎵 **TEACHING TIP**   Play slowly at first and gradually increase the tempo to **Allegro**.

Percussion   Review doubling, or double sticking.

Kybd. Perc.   Remember: Use a slow up-stroke on eighth notes to produce legato style.

138. JOSHUA

African-American Spiritual

180

TEACHING TIP Review the counting of the pick-up notes as they apply to the cut time signature. Also, remind students to hold tied notes for their full value.

139. LISTEN TO THE MOCKINGBIRD

Alice Hawthorne

Percussion Rudiment

Tap Flam

The Tap Flam is simply the reverse of the rudiment Flam Tap. Notice once you get started, this new rudiment feels very much like the Flam Tap. The difference is that you begin this new rudiment with the tap stroke, followed by the flam.

182

TEACHING TIP   Practice the second ending in preparation for this exercise.

140. ANCHORS AWEIGH

Capt. A.H. Miles and C.A. Zimmerman

184

⚡ **TEACHING TIP**   Have students circle the accidentals.

141. GREENSLEEVES

English Folk Song

Electric Bass   Use A♭ major scale fingering.

Kybd. Perc.   Remember: Use a slow up-stroke on eighth notes to produce legato style.

(Ex. 143)
Percussion

Chimes   Use a rawhide mallet or a special hammer with a synthetic head to play the chimes. There is a rounded cap that is placed at the top of each tube; this is the striking area. Always remember to play the instrument on the cap; *never* strike the instrument anywhere else or you will damage the tubes.

186

Clarinet  Clarinet

Percussion   Review paradiddle, triple paradiddle, double paradiddle

🎵 **TEACHING TIP**   Encourage students not to overblow in the higher register and to use good breath support.

142. THE LONG CLIMB – New Notes

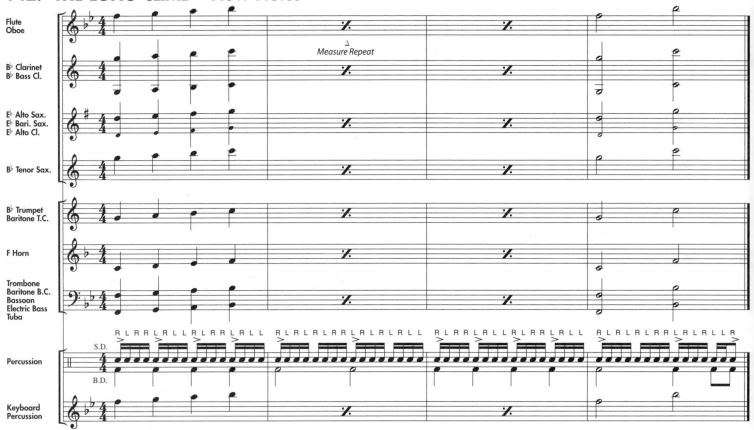

🎵 **TEACHING TIP**   Emphasize good phrasing by encouraging students to breathe only at the breath marks.

143. THE BLUE BELLS OF SCOTLAND

Scottish Folk Song

188

Major and Minor

THEORY

The scales you've already learned are called **Major** scales. They all follow the same pattern, with **half-steps** between notes 3–4 and between notes 7–8.

Natural Minor scales follow a different pattern, with **half-steps** between notes 2–3 and 5–6. The **G Minor** scale uses the same key signature as **B♭ Major**.

Another type of minor scale is called **Harmonic Minor**, which adds an accidental to raise the **7th** note by a half-step. Compare the scales on the right.

See page 37 for additional minor scales.

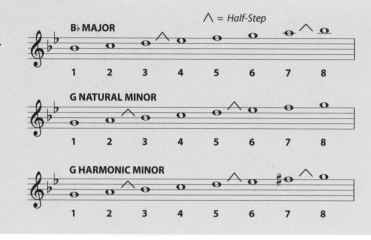

∧ = Half-Step

B♭ MAJOR

G NATURAL MINOR

G HARMONIC MINOR

Bassoon   Trombone   Baritone B.C.   Baritone T.C.   Tuba

 **TEACHING TIP**   Ask students where the half-steps occur.

144. NATURAL MINOR SCALE – New Note

TEACHING TIP Ask students whether this exercise sounds major or minor.

145. FINALE FROM "NEW WORLD SYMPHONY"

Antonin Dvořák

Clarinet

G♯/A♭

TEACHING TIP   Ask students to identify the whole steps *and* the raised seventh step of the scale.

146. HARMONIC MINOR SCALE – New Note

TEACHING TIP Ask students whether this is a major or minor exercise.

147. HUNGARIAN DANCE NO. 5

Johannes Brahms

Student Book Page 30

⚡ **TEACHING TIP**   Ask students whether this is a major or minor exercise.

148. POMP AND CIRCUMSTANCE

Edward Elgar

PERFORMANCE SPOTLIGHT

D.S. al Coda   Play until you see the **D.S. al Coda**. Then go back to the sign (𝄋) and play until the **Coda Sign** ("To Coda" 𝄌). Skip directly to the **Coda** and play until the end.

TEACHING TIP   Explain the **D.S. al Coda** and point out the key change at measure 20.

149. SIMPLE GIFTS – Band Arrangement

Shaker Folk Song
Arr. by John Higgins

Student Book Page 31

⚡ TEACHING TIP   Review 6/8 time. Don't allow rushing and stress proper articulation.

150. SEMPER FIDELIS – Band Arrangement

John Philip Sousa
Arr. by John Higgins

▲   ▲

Percussion
Open Rolls in 6/8   Use eighth note hand motions and play double bounces on the rolls.

38
Flute
Oboe
Bassoon
B♭ Clarinet
E♭ Alto Cl.
B♭ Bass Cl.
E♭ Alto Sax.
B♭ Tenor Sax.
E♭ Bari. Sax.
38
B♭ Trumpet
F Horn
Trombone
Baritone
Tuba
(Electric Bass)
Percussion
Keyboard
Percussion

PERFORMANCE SPOTLIGHT

📚 **TEACHING TIP** The dynamic fortissimo *ff* (play very loud) is used in measure 26. Instruct your students to use good breath support and tone quality when playing loudly, and not to overblow.

Irish Folk Song
Arr. by John Higgins

151. DANNY BOY – Band Arrangement

Student Book Page 32

212

TEACHING TIP   Try conducting in "one" to get the proper feel.

152. TAKE ME OUT TO THE BALL GAME – Band Arrangement

By Jack Norworth and Harry von Tilzer
Arr. by John Higgins

Student Book Page 32

PERFORMANCE SPOTLIGHT

TEACHING TIP Ask students where the time and key changes occur. Discuss measures 49–57, making sure students understand when they are supposed to play.

153. SERENGETI (AFRICAN RHAPSODY) – Band Arrangement

John Higgins

Percussion
Wind Chimes — Wind Chimes are varying lengths of a brass or metal alloy hung from a short wooden bar. They are played by gently sweeping the hand along the line of strung tubes, generally from the high to low end.

224

RUBANK® STUDIES

 **TEACHING TIP**

The following supplemental exercises have multiple uses as needed. They are excellent for expanding individual technical skills, and may be introduced as extra challenges when appropriate for individual players. They can also be used as full band warm-ups and technique builders. Additional performance skills can be reinforced by varying the tempo, dynamics, etc.

154. CHORALE (Concert B♭)

155. CHORALE (Concert E♭)

234

156. CHORALE (Concert F)

157. CHORALE (Concert A♭)

236

158. CHORALE (Concert C)

KEY OF CONCERT B♭ MAJOR

159.

238

KEY OF B♭

160.

KEY OF B♭
161.

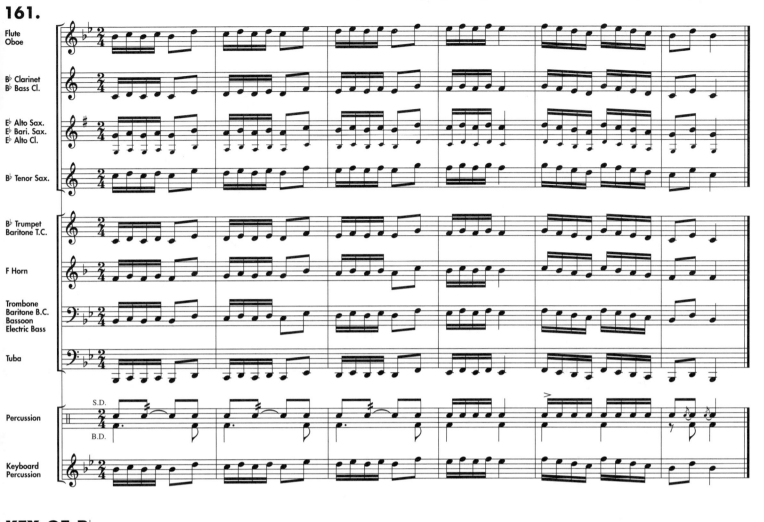

KEY OF B♭
162.

RUBANK® STUDIES

KEY OF CONCERT E♭ MAJOR **Electric Bass** Use E♭ major scale fingering.

163.

KEY OF E♭   **Electric Bass**   Use E♭ major scale fingering.

164.

242

KEY OF E♭
165.

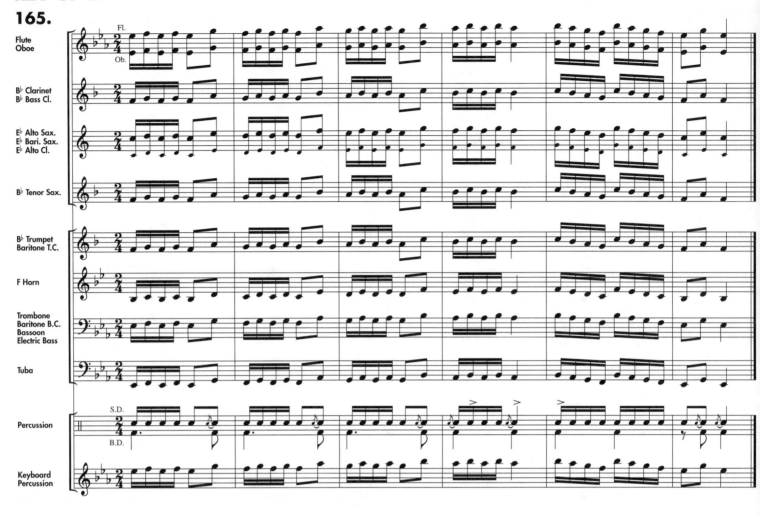

KEY OF E♭   **Electric Bass** Use E♭ major scale fingering.
166.

KEY OF CONCERT F MAJOR   **Electric Bass** Use F major scale fingering.

167.

KEY OF F

168.

KEY OF F

169.

KEY OF F

Electric Bass Use F major scale fingering.

170.

RUBANK® STUDIES

KEY OF CONCERT A♭ MAJOR   **Electric Bass** Use A♭ major scale fingering.

171.

248

KEY OF A♭   **Electric Bass** Use A♭ major scale fingering.

172.

KEY OF A♭   **Electric Bass**   Use A♭ major scale fingering.

173.

KEY OF A♭   **Electric Bass**   Use A♭ major scale fingering.

174.

KEY OF CONCERT C MAJOR

175.

KEY OF C

Electric Bass Try without using open strings.

176.

KEY OF C

177.

Flute
Oboe

B♭ Clarinet
B♭ Bass Cl.

E♭ Alto Sax.
E♭ Bari. Sax.
E♭ Alto Cl.

B♭ Tenor Sax.

B♭ Trumpet
Baritone T.C.

F Horn

Trombone
Baritone B.C.
Bassoon
Electric Bass

Tuba

Percussion

Keyboard
Percussion

KEY OF C
178.

RUBANK® STUDIES

KEY OF CONCERT G MINOR

179.

KEY OF G MINOR

180.

KEY OF CONCERT C MINOR

181.

KEY OF C MINOR

182.

KEY OF CONCERT D MINOR

183.

KEY OF D MINOR

184.

CHROMATIC SCALES

185.

CHROMATIC SCALES
186.

Flute

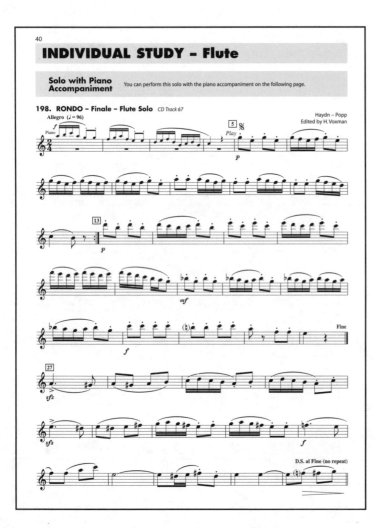

Oboe

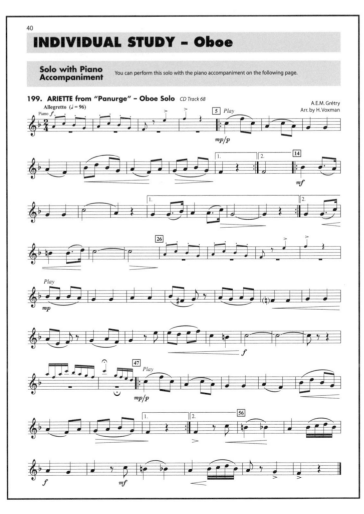

264

Bassoon

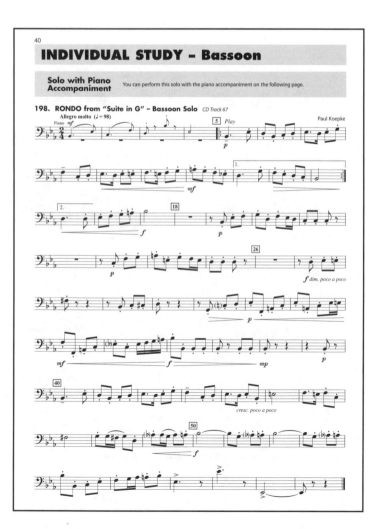

Clarinet

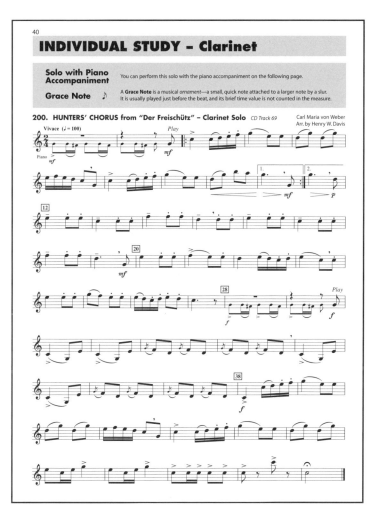

266

Alto Clarinet

Bass Clarinet

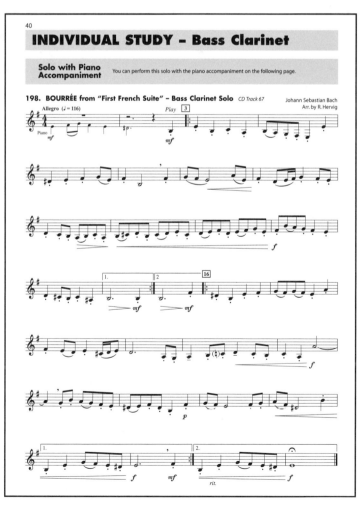

268

Alto Saxophone

Tenor Saxophone

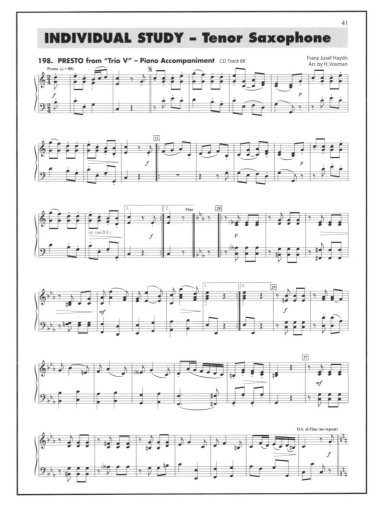

Baritone Saxophone

Trumpet

272

F Horn

Trombone

274

Baritone B.C.

Baritone T.C.

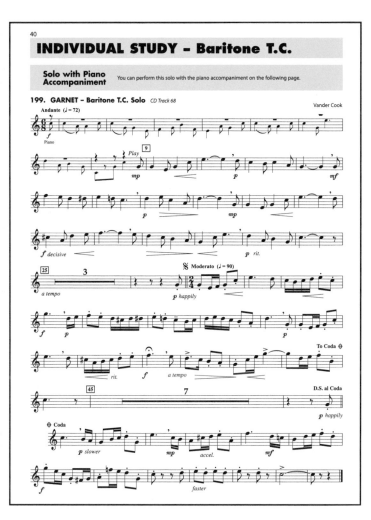

276

Student Book Pages 38–41

Tuba

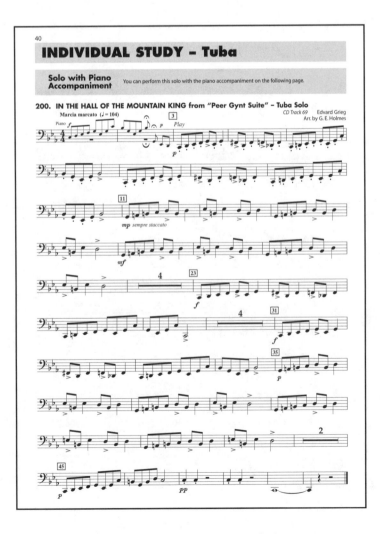

Electric Bass

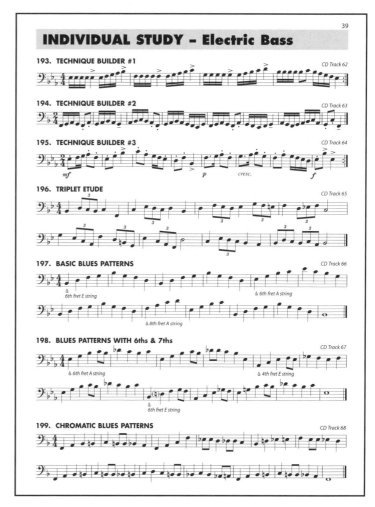

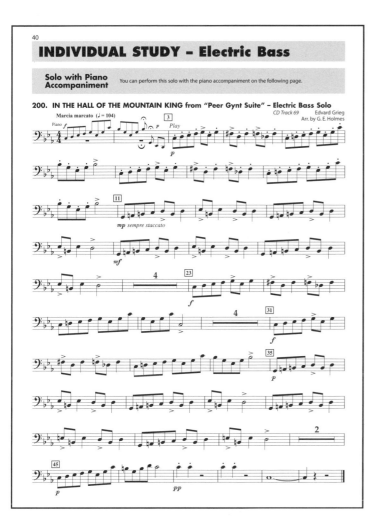

278

Percussion

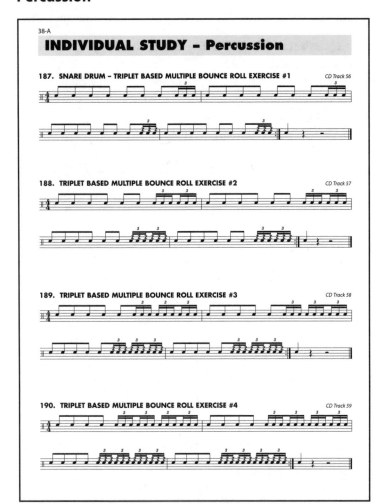

Percussion

Keyboard Percussion

Keyboard Percussion

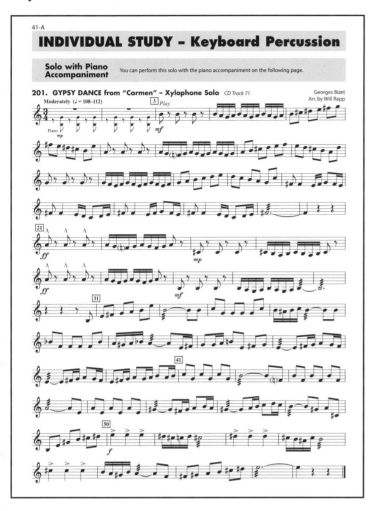

RHYTHM STUDIES

TEACHING TIP The use of these supplementary rhythm exercises should be started in the early stages of a student's development. They advance sequentially, and can be used in any length of measure groupings. By specifying how often to change pitch, they can become very challenging.

RHYTHM STUDIES

CREATING MUSIC

Theme and Variation

Theme and Variation is a technique used by composers and arrangers to create interesting musical ideas that are "varied" from an established melody, or "theme." Play the following theme and two variations to hear how the arranger has created new phrases based on the original melody.

1. THEME

"Simple Gifts"

VARIATION 1 *Adding some notes • Changing some rhythms*

VARIATION 2 *Removing notes • Changing rhythms • Adding accents • Adding notes*

2. THEME AND YOUR VARIATION

Write your own variation of this theme. Use your instrument to hear and try different ideas.

"Oh, Susanna"

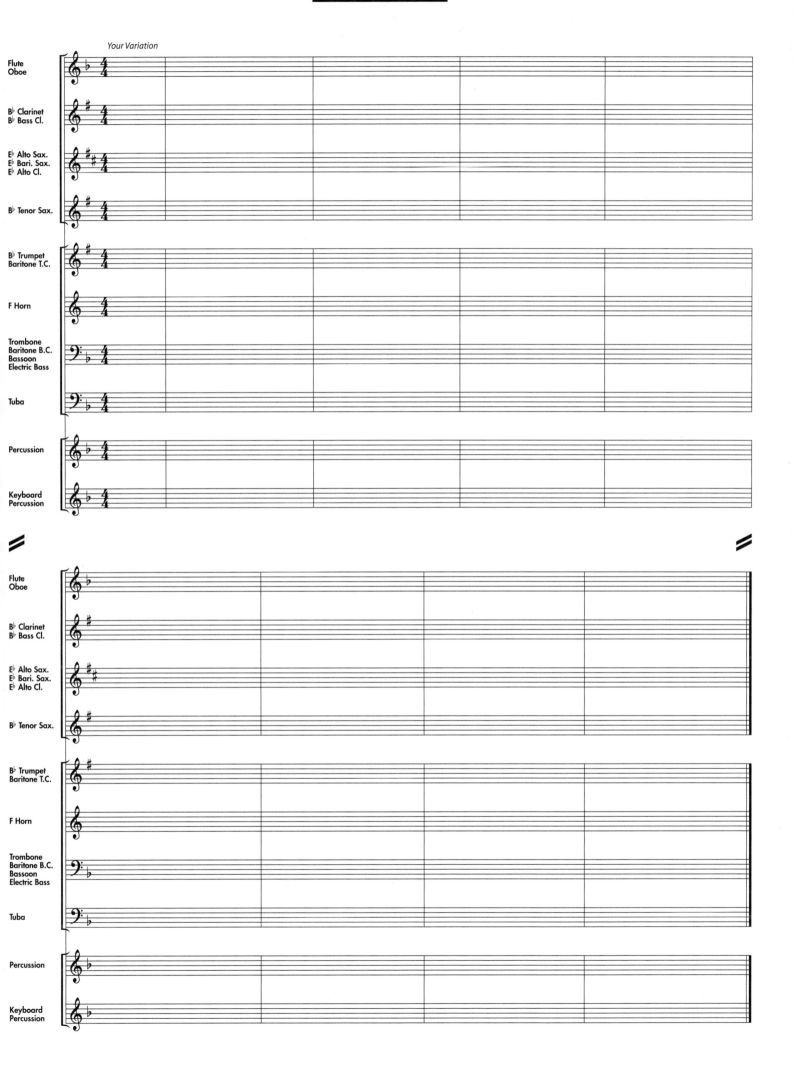

288

THEORY

Blues Improvisation

Improvisation using a **Blues Scale** is an important part of jazz and popular music. Musicians use combinations of these notes and various rhythms to create their own spontaneous solos over a 12 measure progression of chords.

Blues Scale

3. LET'S JAM *Use the indicated notes from the Blues Scale to create your own solo to play with the accompaniment (Line B).*

290

You can mark your progress through the book on this page. Fill in the stars as instructed by your band director.

ESSENTIAL ELEMENTS 2000

STAR ACHIEVER

NAME_____

1. Page 2–4, Review
2. Page 5, Sightreading Challenge, No. 19
3. Page 6, Daily Warm-Ups
4. Page 7, Sightreading Challenge, No. 31
5. Page 8, Essential Creativity, No. 38
6. Page 9, EE Quiz, No. 43
7. Page 10, Sightreading Challenge, No. 49
8. Page 11, EE Quiz, No. 55
9. Page 12–13, Performance Spotlight
10. Page 15, EE Quiz, No. 74
11. Page 16, Sightreading Challenge, No. 80
12. Page 18, Daily Warm-Ups
13. Page 19, Essential Creativity, No. 96
14. Page 20, Sightreading Challenge, No. 100

15. Page 21, EE Quiz, No. 106
16. Page 22, Chromatic Scale, No. 107
17. Page 23, Sightreading Challenge, No. 115
18. Page 24, EE Quiz, No. 120
19. Page 25, EE Quiz, No. 126
20. Page 27, EE Quiz, No. 133
21. Page 30, Natural Minor Scale, No. 144
22. Page 30, Harmonic Minor Scale, No. 146
23. Page 30, Pomp and Circumstance, No. 148
24. Page 31, Performance Spotlight
25. Page 32, Performance Spotlight
26. Page 33, Performance Spotlight
27. Page 38–39, Individual Study
28. Page 40, Performance Spotlight

MUSIC — AN ESSENTIAL ELEMENT OF LIFE

FINGERING CHART   **FLUTE**

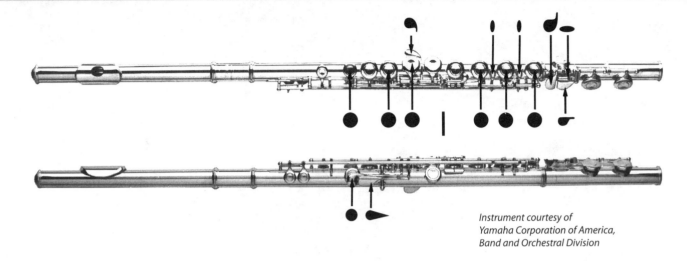

Instrument courtesy of
Yamaha Corporation of America,
Band and Orchestral Division

○ = Open
● = Pressed down

The most common fingering appears
first when two fingerings are shown.

Instrument Care Reminders

Before putting your instrument back in its case after playing, do the following:

- Draw a cleaning cloth and rod through the middle and foot joints, and into the head joint.
- Carefully wipe the outside of each section to keep the finish clean. Don't try to polish between the keys. Let a repair specialist do this for you when needed.

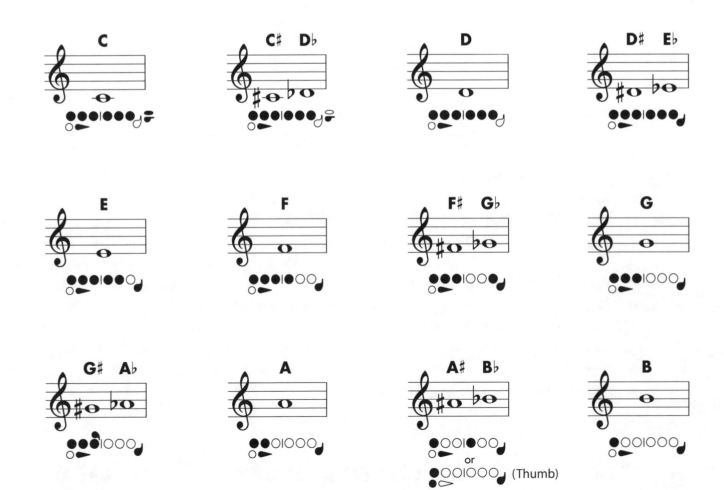

FINGERING CHART

FLUTE

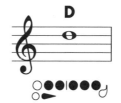

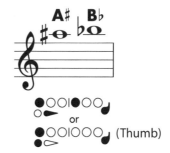

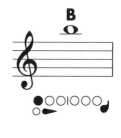

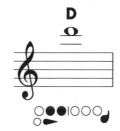

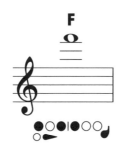

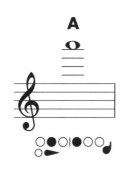

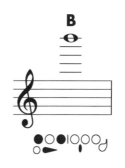

FINGERING CHART

Instrument Care Reminders

Before putting your instrument back
in its case after playing, do the following:

- Carefully remove the reed and blow air
  through it from the bottom to the top.
  Return to reed case.
- Take the instrument apart in the reverse
  order of assembly. Swab out each section
  with a cloth or feather swab. If the cloth
  swab has a weight on one end, drop the
  weight through and pull until you feel a
  slight resistance. Then pull the swab back
  out from the bottom. Never try to pull the
  swab all the way through the top section.
  Return each section to the correct spot in
  the case.

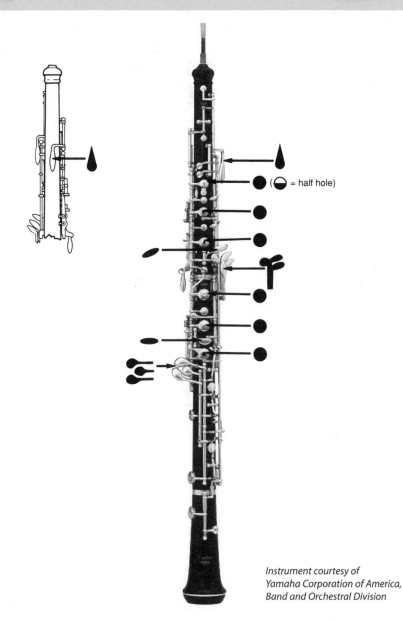

(◒ = half hole)

○ = Open
● = Pressed down
◒ = Half hole covered

*Instrument courtesy of
Yamaha Corporation of America,
Band and Orchestral Division*

 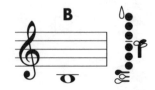 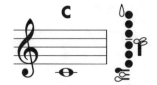 

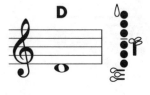 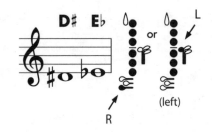 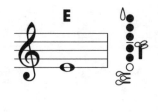 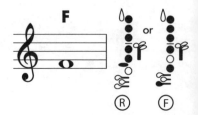

FINGERING CHART

OBOE

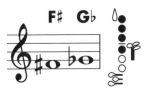

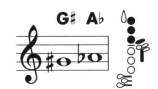

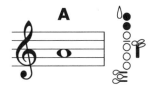

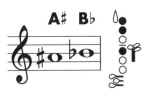

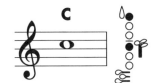

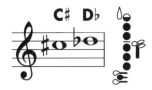

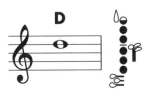

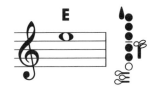

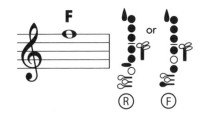

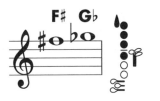

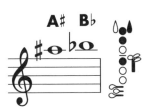

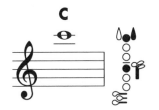

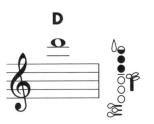

FINGERING CHART

Instrument Care Reminders

Before putting your instrument back in its case after playing, do the following:

- Carefully remove the reed and blow air through the bottom of it. Return to reed case.
- Remove the bocal and blow air through the cork end to remove excess moisture.
- Take the instrument apart in the reverse order of assembly. Swab out each section with a cloth swab or cleaning rod. Drop the weight of the swab through the bottom end and pull it through. Return each section to the correct spot in the case.

○ = Open
● = Pressed down
◑ = Half-hole covered

The most common fingering appears first when two fingerings are shown.

Instrument courtesy of Yamaha Corporation of America, Band and Orchestral Division

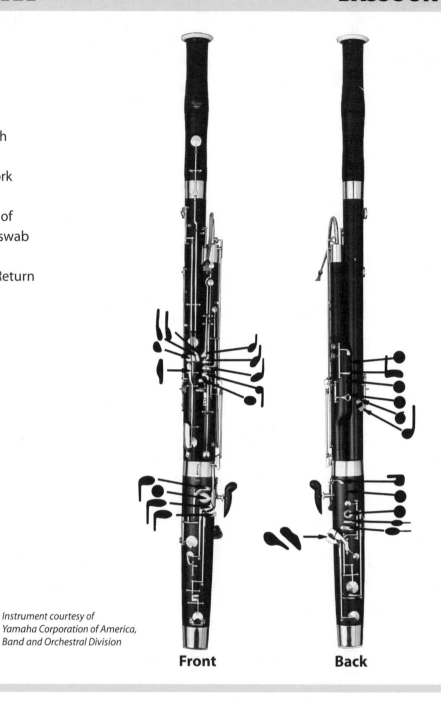

Front   **Back**

A♯ B♭

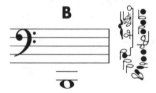

B

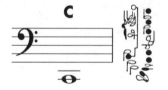

C

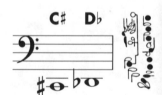

C♯ D♭

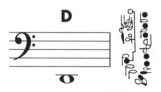

D

D♯ E♭

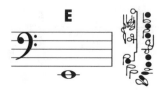

E

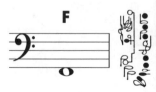

F

FINGERING CHART

BASSOON

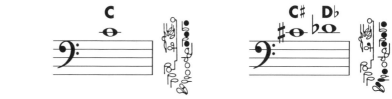

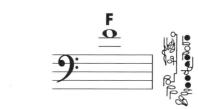

FINGERING CHART

Bb CLARINET

Instrument Care Reminders

Before putting your instrument back in its case after playing, do the following:

- Remove the reed, wipe off excess moisture.
- Remove the mouthpiece and wipe the inside with a clean cloth. Place the reed back on the mouthpiece.
- Hold the upper section with your left hand and the lower section with your right hand. Gently twist the sections apart. Shake out the excess moisture.
- Drop the weighted chamois or cotton swab into each section and pull it out the bottom.
- Carefully twist the barrel and bell from each section. Dry off any additional moisture.
- As you put each piece back in the case, check to be sure they are dry.
- Your case is designed to hold only specific objects. If you try to force anything else into the case, it may damage your instrument.

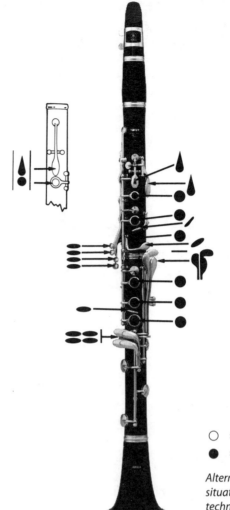

○ = Open
● = Pressed down

Alternate fingerings are used in certain situations to allow for smoother technique. These are shown to the right of the more common fingerings.

Instrument courtesy of Yamaha Corporation of America, Band and Orchestral Division

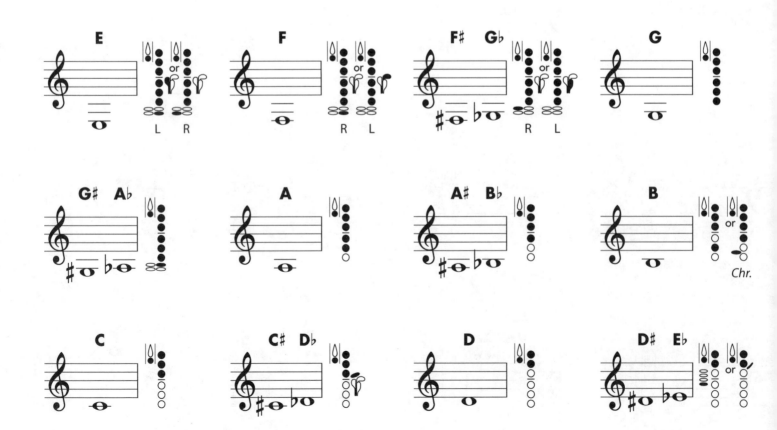

FINGERING CHART

B♭ CLARINET

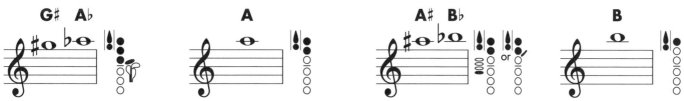

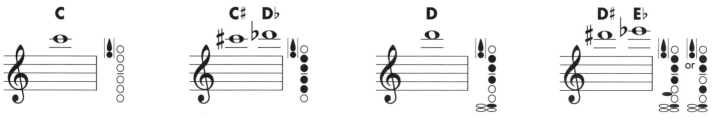

FINGERING CHART

Eb ALTO CLARINET

Instrument Care Reminders

Before putting your instrument back in its case after playing, do the following:

- Remove the reed, wipe off excess moisture.
- Remove the mouthpiece and wipe the inside with a clean cloth. Place the reed back on the mouthpiece.
- Hold the upper section with your left hand and the lower section with your right hand. Gently twist the sections apart. Shake out the excess moisture.
- Drop the weighted chamois or cotton swab into each section and pull it out the bottom.
- Carefully twist the barrel and bell from each section. Dry off any additional moisture.
- As you put each piece back in the case, check to be sure they are dry.
- Your case is designed to hold only specific objects. If you try to force anything else into the case, it may damage your instrument.

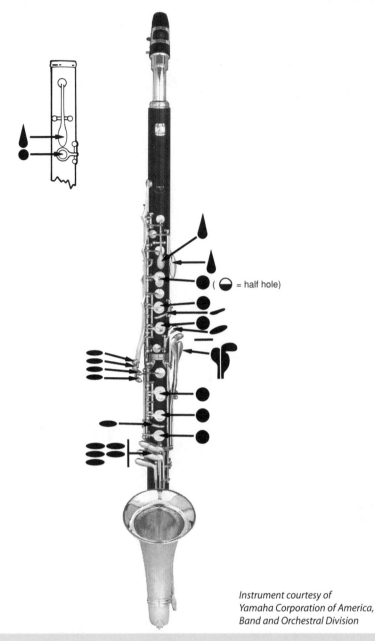

(◐ = half hole)

○ = Open
● = Pressed down

Alternate fingerings are used in certain situations to allow for smoother technique. These are shown to the right of the more common fingerings.

*Instrument courtesy of
Yamaha Corporation of America,
Band and Orchestral Division*

FINGERING CHART

E♭ ALTO CLARINET

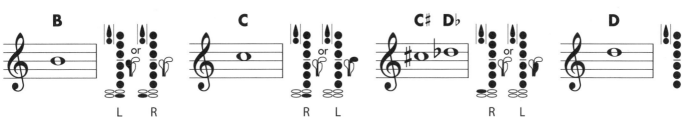

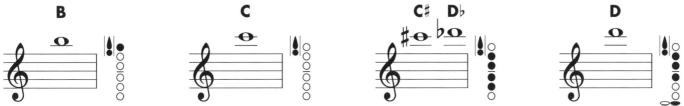

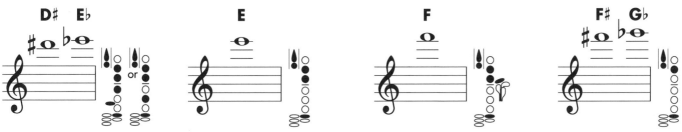

FINGERING CHART

Bb BASS CLARINET

Instrument Care Reminders

Before putting your instrument back in its case after playing, do the following:

- Remove the reed, wipe off excess moisture.
- Remove the mouthpiece and wipe the inside with a clean cloth. Place the reed back on the mouthpiece.
- Hold the upper section with your left hand and the lower section with your right hand. Gently twist the sections apart. Shake out the excess moisture.
- Drop the weighted chamois or cotton swab into each section and pull it out the bottom.
- Carefully twist the barrel and bell from each section. Dry off any additional moisture.
- As you put each piece back in the case, check to be sure they are dry.
- Your case is designed to hold only specific objects. If you try to force anything else into the case, it may damage your instrument.

○ = Open
● = Pressed down

Alternate fingerings are used in certain situations to allow for smoother technique. These are shown to the right of the more common fingerings.

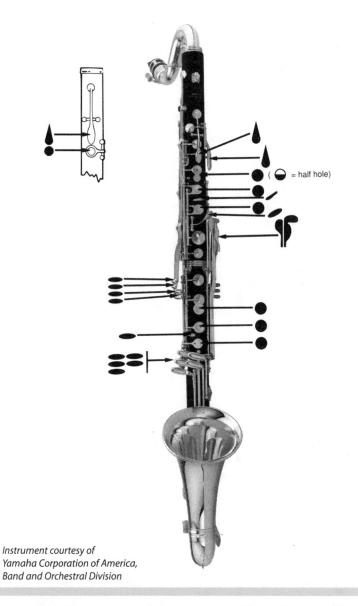

(⬭ = half hole)

Instrument courtesy of Yamaha Corporation of America, Band and Orchestral Division

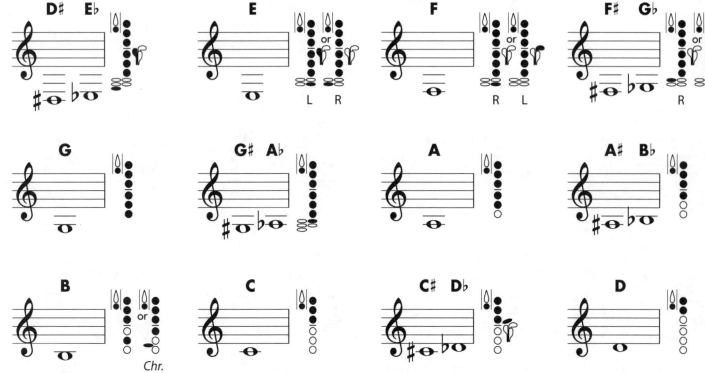

FINGERING CHART

Bb BASS CLARINET

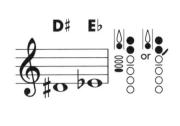

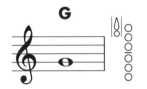

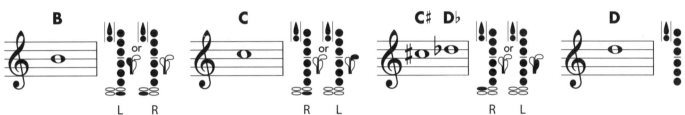
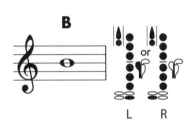
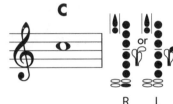

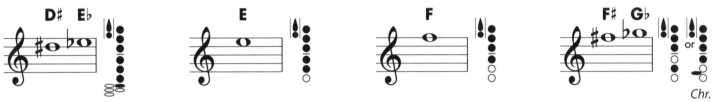

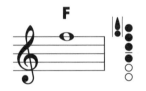

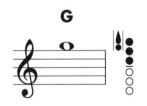

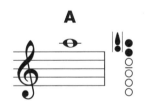

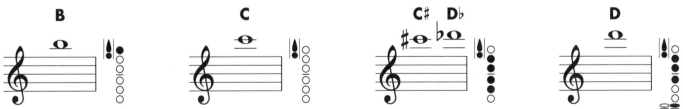
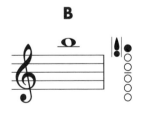

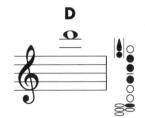

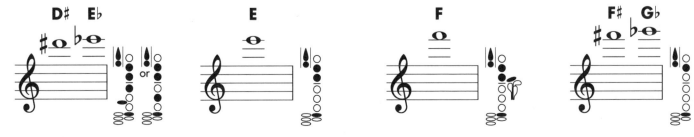
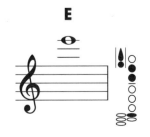

FINGERING CHART

E♭ ALTO SAXOPHONE

Instrument Care Reminders

Before putting your instrument back in its case after playing, do the following:

- Remove the reed, wipe off excess moisture.
- Remove the mouthpiece and wipe the inside with a clean cloth.
- Place reed back onto mouthpiece.
- Remove the neck and shake out excess moisture. Dry with a rolled up paper towel.
- Drop the weight of the chamois or cotton swab into the bell. Pull the swab through the body several times. Return the instrument to its case.
- Your case is designed to hold only specific objects. If you try to force anything else into the case, it may damage your instrument.

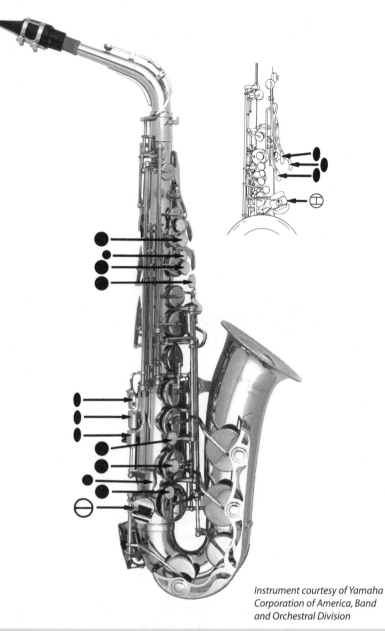

○ = Open
● = Pressed down

The most common fingering appears first when two fingerings are shown.

Instrument courtesy of Yamaha Corporation of America, Band and Orchestral Division

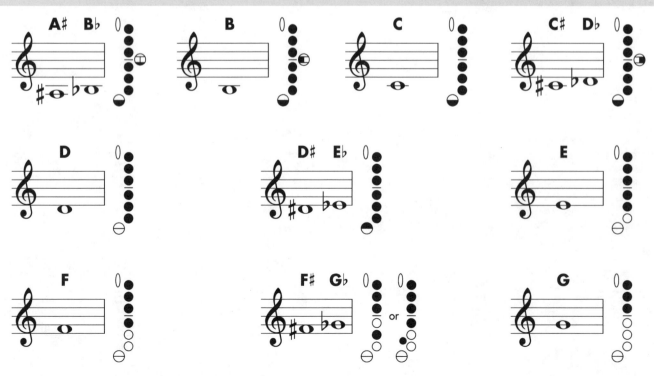

FINGERING CHART

E♭ ALTO SAXOPHONE

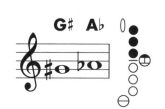
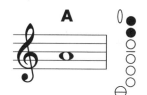
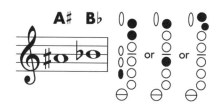
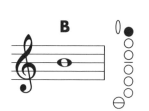
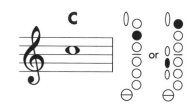

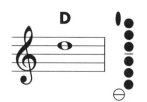

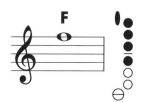
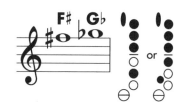

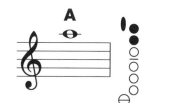
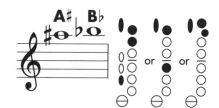
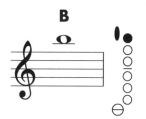
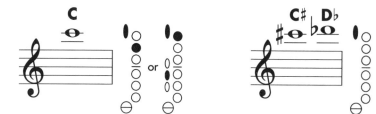

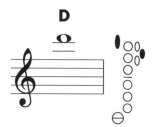

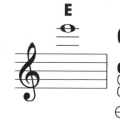

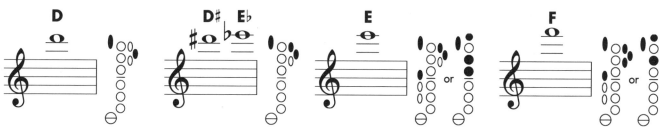

Student Book Page 46

FINGERING CHART

Bb TENOR SAXOPHONE

Instrument Care Reminders

Before putting your instrument back in its case after playing, do the following:

- Remove the reed, wipe off excess moisture.
- Remove the mouthpiece and wipe the inside with a clean cloth.
- Place reed back onto mouthpiece.
- Remove the neck and shake out excess moisture. Dry with a rolled up paper towel.
- Drop the weight of the chamois or cotton swab into the bell. Pull the swab through the body several times. Return the instrument to its case.
- Your case is designed to hold only specific objects. If you try to force anything else into the case, it may damage your instrument.

○ = Open
● = Pressed down

The most common fingering appears first when two fingerings are shown.

Instrument courtesy of Yamaha Corporation of America, Band and Orchestral Division

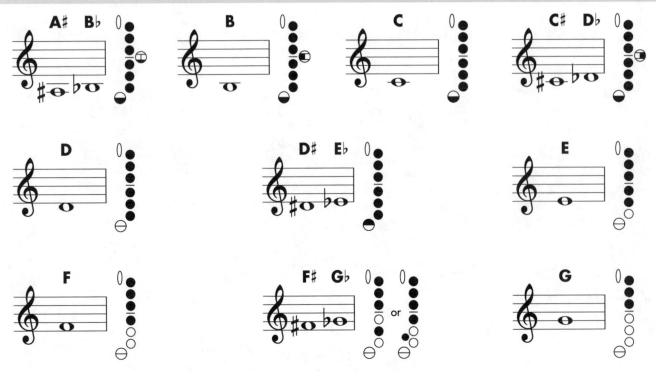

FINGERING CHART

B♭ TENOR SAXOPHONE

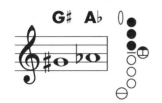

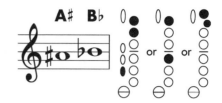
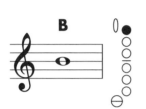
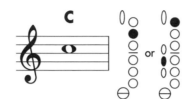

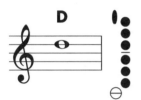

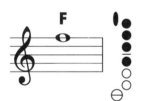

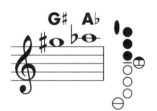
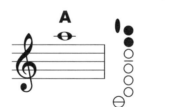
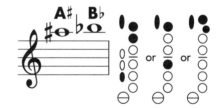
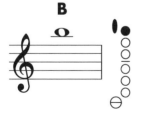
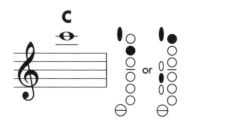

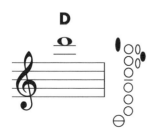
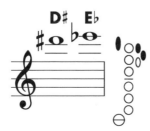

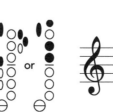
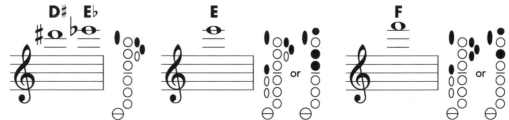

FINGERING CHART

E♭ BARITONE SAXOPHONE

Instrument Care Reminders

Before putting your instrument back in its case after playing, do the following:

- Remove the reed, wipe off excess moisture.
- Remove the mouthpiece and wipe the inside with a clean cloth.
- Place reed back onto mouthpiece.
- Remove the neck and shake out excess moisture. Dry with a rolled up paper towel.
- Drop the weight of the chamois or cotton swab into the bell. Pull the swab through the body several times. Return the instrument to its case.
- Your case is designed to hold only specific objects. If you try to force anything else into the case, it may damage your instrument.

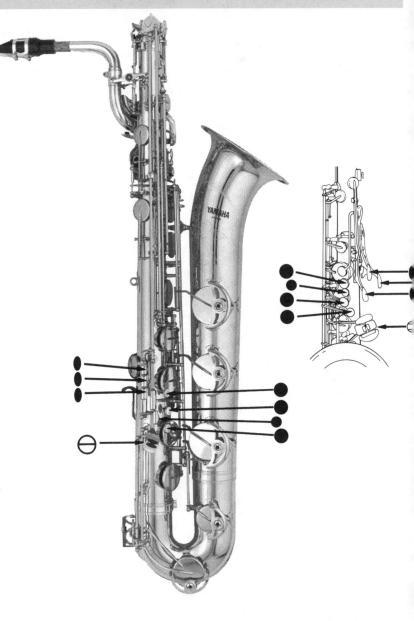

○ = Open

● = Pressed down

The most common fingering appears first when two fingerings are shown.

Instrument courtesy of Yamaha Corporation of America, Band and Orchestral Division

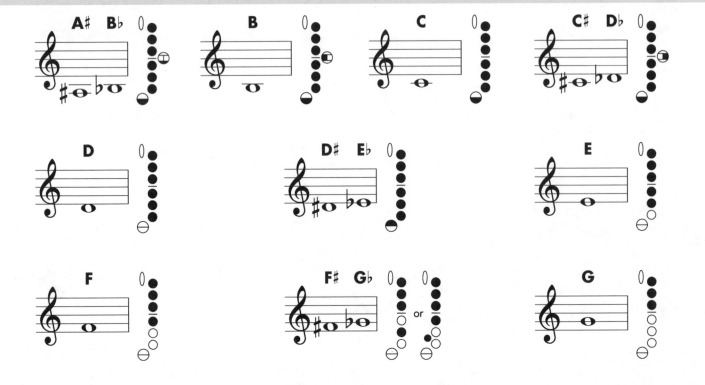

FINGERING CHART   Eb BARITONE SAXOPHONE

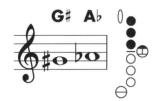

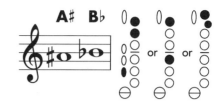

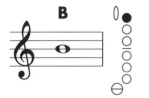

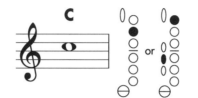

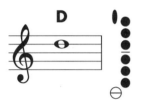

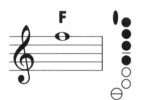

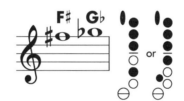

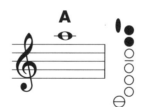

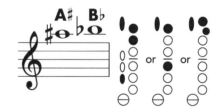

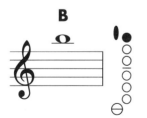

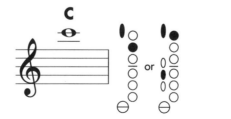

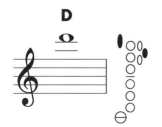

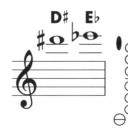

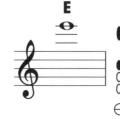

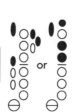

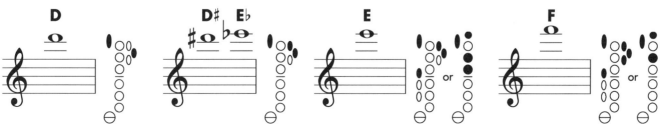

FINGERING CHART

Bb TRUMPET/Bb CORNET

Instrument Care Reminders

Before putting your instrument back in its case after playing, do the following:

- Use the water key to empty water from the instrument. Blow air through it.
- Remove the mouthpiece. Once a week, wash the mouthpiece with warm tap water. Dry thoroughly.
- Wipe off the instrument with a clean soft cloth. Return the instrument to its case.

Trumpet valves occasionally need oiling. To oil your trumpet valves:

- Unscrew the valve at the top of the casing.
- Lift the valve half-way out of the casing.
- Apply a few drops of special brass valve oil to the exposed valve.
- Carefully return the valve to its casing. When properly inserted, the top of the valve should easily screw back into place.

Be sure to grease the slides regularly. Your director will recommend special slide grease and valve oil, and will help you apply them when necessary.

CAUTION: If a slide, a valve or your mouthpiece becomes stuck, ask for help from your band director or music dealer. Special tools should be used to prevent damage to your instrument.

1 2 3

Bb TRUMPET
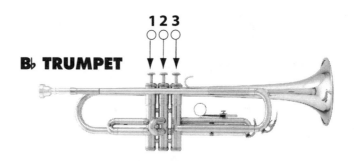

1 2 3

Bb CORNET

○ = Open
● = Pressed down

Instruments courtesy of Yamaha Corporation of America, Band and Orchestral Division

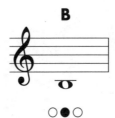

FINGERING CHART

B♭ TRUMPET/B♭ CORNET

D

D♯ E♭

E

F

F♯ G♭

G

G♯ A♭

A

A♯ B♭

B

C

C♯ D♭

D

D♯ E♭

E

F

F♯ G♭

G

G♯ A♭

A

A♯ B♭

B

C

FINGERING CHART

F HORN

Instrument Care Reminders

Before putting your instrument back in its case after playing, do the following:

- Use the water key to empty water from the instrument. Blow air through it. If your horn does not have a water key, invert the instrument. You may also remove the main tuning slide, invert the instrument and remove excess water.
- Wipe the instrument off with a clean soft cloth. Return the instrument to its case.
- Remove the mouthpiece. Once a week, wash the mouthpiece with warm tap water. Dry thoroughly.

Be sure to grease the slides regularly. Your director will recommend special slide grease and valve oil, and will help you apply them when necessary.

CAUTION: If a slide, a valve or your mouthpiece becomes stuck, ask for help from your band director or music dealer. Special tools should be used to prevent damage to your instrument.

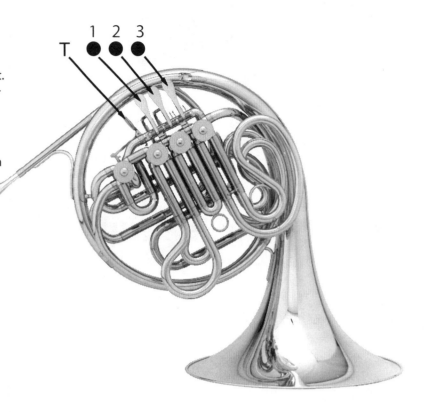

Using the Correct Fingering

F Horn players:
- Use the upper fingerings.

Double Horn players:
- Use the lower "**T**" fingerings when indicated. It is easier to play notes in the upper and extreme lower register of the horn using these fingerings.

B♭ Horn players:
- Use the lower fingerings. The "**T**" key is only used on double horns.

○ = Open
● = Pressed down

Instrument courtesy of Yamaha Corporation of America, Band and Orchestral Division

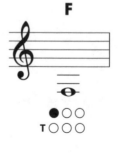

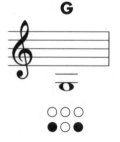
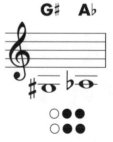
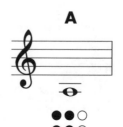

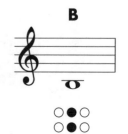

FINGERING CHART

F HORN

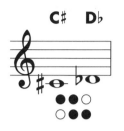

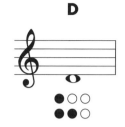

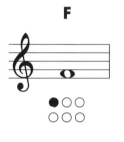

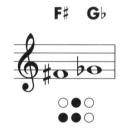

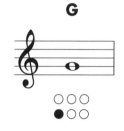

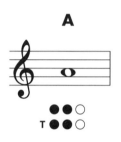

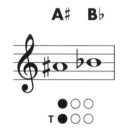

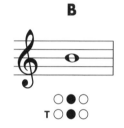

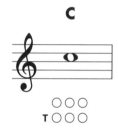

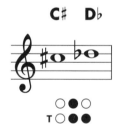

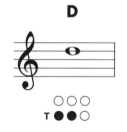

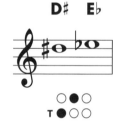

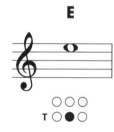

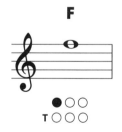

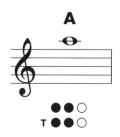

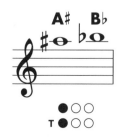

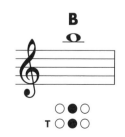

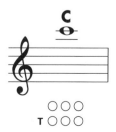

POSITION CHART   TROMBONE

Numbers below the notes = Slide positions

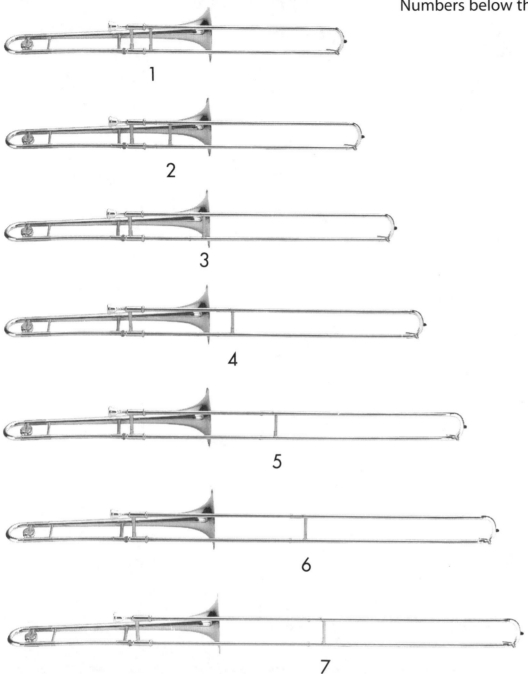

Instrument courtesy of
Yamaha Corporation of America,
Band and Orchestral Division

Instrument Care Reminders

Before putting your instrument back in its case after playing, do the following:

- Use the water key to empty water from the instrument. Blow air through it.
- Remove the mouthpiece and slide assembly. Do not take the outer slide off the inner slide piece. Return the instrument to its case.
- Once a week, wash the mouthpiece with warm tap water. Dry thoroughly.

Trombone slides occasionally need oiling. To oil your slide, simply:

- Rest the tip of the slide on the floor and unlock the slide.
- Exposing the inner slide, put a few drops of oil on the inner slide.
- Rapidly move the slide back and forth. The oil will then lubricate the slide.
- Be sure to grease the tuning slide regularly. Your director will recommend special slide oil and grease, and will help you apply them when necessary.

CAUTION: If a slide or your mouthpiece becomes stuck, ask for help from your band director or music dealer. Special tools should be used to prevent damage to your instrument.

POSITION CHART   **TROMBONE**

E	F	F# Gb	G
	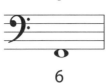		
7	6	5	4

G# Ab	A	A# Bb	B
		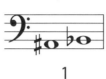	
3	2	1	7

C	C# Db	D	D# Eb
		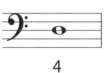	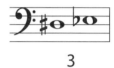
6	5	4	3

E	F	F# Gb	G
	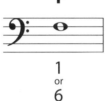	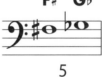	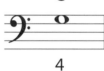
2	1 or 6	5	4

G# Ab	A	A# Bb	B
		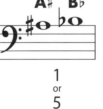	
3	2 or 6	1 or 5	4

C	C# Db	D	D# Eb
		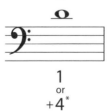	
3	2	1 or +4*	3

E	F	F# Gb	G
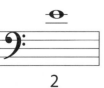		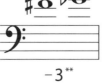	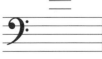
2	1	−3**	−2

* + = Make the slide a little longer.
** − = Make the slide a little shorter.

FINGERING CHART   BARITONE B.C.

Instrument Care Reminders

Before putting your instrument back in its case after playing, do the following:

*   Use the water key to empty water from the instrument. Blow air through it.
*   Remove the mouthpiece. Once a week, wash the mouthpiece with warm tap water. Dry thoroughly.
*   Wipe off the instrument with a clean soft cloth. Return the instrument to its case.

Baritone valves occasionally need oiling. To oil your baritone valves:

*   Unscrew the valve at the top of the casing.
*   Lift the valve half-way out of the casing.
*   Apply a few drops of special brass valve oil to the exposed valve.
*   Carefully return the valve to its casing. When properly inserted, the top of the valve should easily screw back into place.

Be sure to grease the slides regularly. Your director will recommend special slide grease and valve oil, and will help you apply them when necessary.

CAUTION: If a slide, a valve or your mouthpiece becomes stuck, ask for help from your band director or music dealer. Special tools should be used to prevent damage to your instrument.

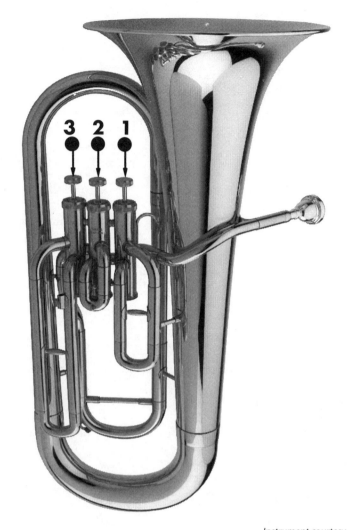

○ = Open
● = Pressed down

*Instrument courtesy of
Yamaha Corporation of America,
Band and Orchestral Division*

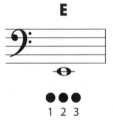

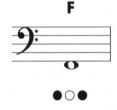

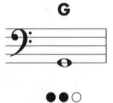

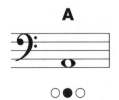

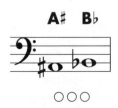

FINGERING CHART

BARITONE B.C.

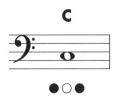

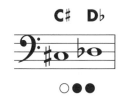

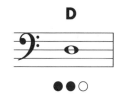

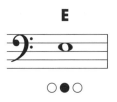

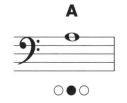

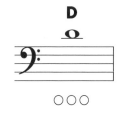

FINGERING CHART

Instrument Care Reminders

Before putting your instrument back in its case after playing, do the following:

- Use the water key to empty water from the instrument. Blow air through it.
- Remove the mouthpiece. Once a week, wash the mouthpiece with warm tap water. Dry thoroughly.
- Wipe off the instrument with a clean soft cloth. Return the instrument to its case.

Baritone valves occasionally need oiling. To oil your baritone valves:

- Unscrew the valve at the top of the casing.
- Lift the valve half-way out of the casing.
- Apply a few drops of special brass valve oil to the exposed valve.
- Carefully return the valve to its casing. When properly inserted, the top of the valve should easily screw back into place.

Be sure to grease the slides regularly. Your director will recommend special slide grease and valve oil, and will help you apply them when necessary.

CAUTION: If a slide, a valve or your mouthpiece becomes stuck, ask for help from your band director or music dealer. Special tools should be used to prevent damage to your instrument.

○ = Open
● = Pressed down

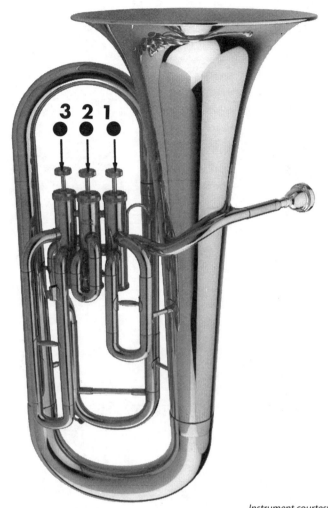

Instrument courtesy of Yamaha Corporation of America, Band and Orchestral Division

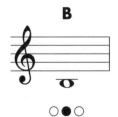

FINGERING CHART

BARITONE T.C.

FINGERING CHART

TUBA

Instrument Care Reminders

Before putting your instrument back in its case after playing, do the following:

- Use the water key to empty water from the instrument. Blow air through it.
- Remove the mouthpiece. Once a week, wash the mouthpiece with warm tap water. Dry thoroughly.
- Wipe off the instrument with a clean soft cloth. Return the instrument to its case.

Tuba valves occasionally need oiling. To oil your valves, simply:

- Unscrew the valve at the top of the casing.
- Lift the valve half-way out of the casing.
- Apply a few drops of oil to the exposed metal valve.
- Carefully return the valve to its casing. When properly inserted, the top of the valve should easily screw back into place.

Be sure to grease the slides regularly. Your director will recommend special slide grease and valve oil, and will help you apply them when necessary.

CAUTION: If a slide, a valve or your mouthpiece becomes stuck, ask for help from your band director or music dealer. Special tools should be used to prevent damage to your instrument.

○ = Open
● = Pressed down

Instrument courtesy of Yamaha Corporation of America, Band and Orchestral Division

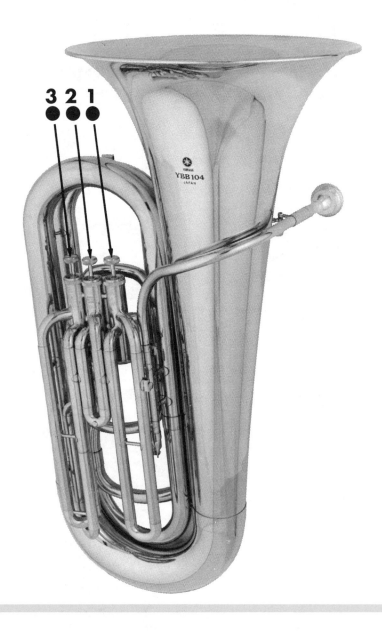

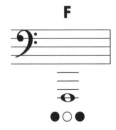

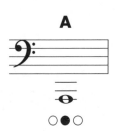
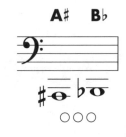
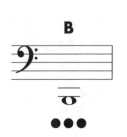

FINGERING CHART

TUBA

C
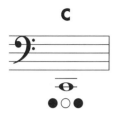

C♯ D♭
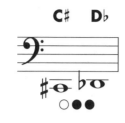

D
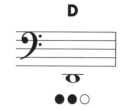

D♯ E♭

E
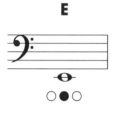

F
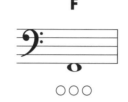

F♯ G♭

G
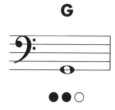

G♯ A♭

A
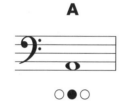

A♯ B♭
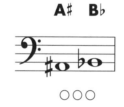

B
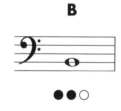

C

C♯ D♭
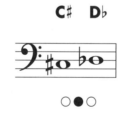

D
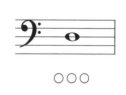

D♯ E♭

E

F

F♯ G♭

G

G♯ A♭

A
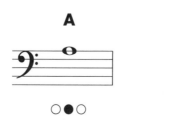

A♯ B♭

FINGERING CHART

ELECTRIC BASS

Instrument Care Reminders

- Be sure your amplifier is turned off before plugging-in or unplugging the audio cable connecting it to your instrument.
- When unplugging a cable, hold it by the plug (not by the wire).
- After playing, wipe off the instrument and strings with a clean soft cloth. Return the instrument to its case.
- Close all the latches on your case when the instrument is inside.
- Keep all 4 strings in tune (at normal tension) to prevent warping of the neck.
- Your case is designed to hold only specific objects. If you force anything else into the case, it may damage your instrument.

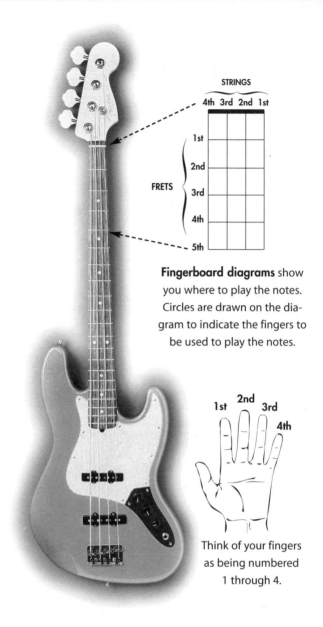

Fingerboard diagrams show you where to play the notes. Circles are drawn on the diagram to indicate the fingers to be used to play the notes.

Think of your fingers as being numbered 1 through 4.

Instrument courtesy of Yamaha Corporation of America, Band and Orchestral Division

E

F

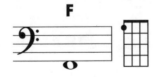

F♯ G♭

G

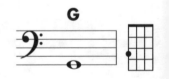

G♯ A♭

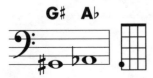

A

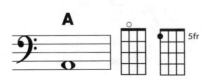

A♯ B♭

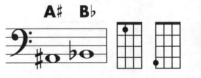

FINGERING CHART

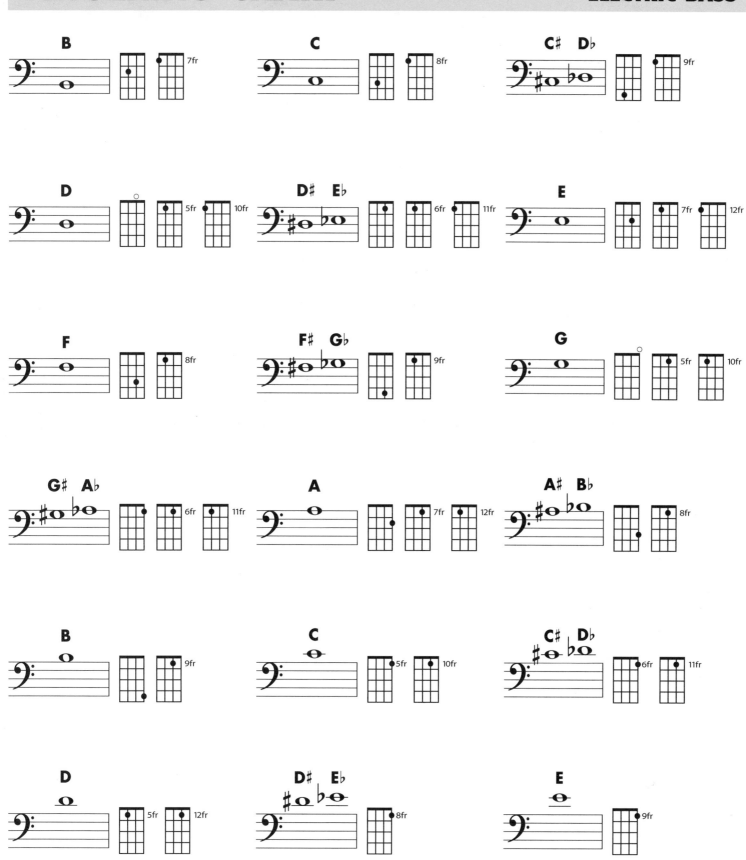

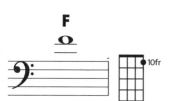

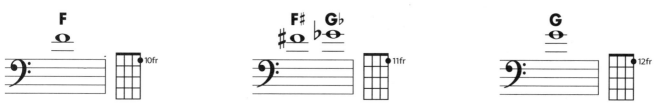

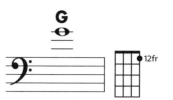

SNARE DRUM INTERNATIONAL DRUM RUDIMENTS

All rudiments should be practiced: open (slow) to close (fast) and/or at an even moderate march tempo.

Instrument Care Reminders

Snare drums occasionally need tuning. Ask your teacher to help you tighten each tension rod equally using a drum key.

- Be careful not to over-tighten the head. It will break if the tension is too tight.
- Loosen the snare strainer at the end of each rehearsal.
- Cover all percussion instruments when not in use.
- Put sticks away in a storage area. Keep the percussion section neat!
- Sticks are the only things which should be placed on the snare drum. NEVER put or allow others to put objects on any percussion instrument.

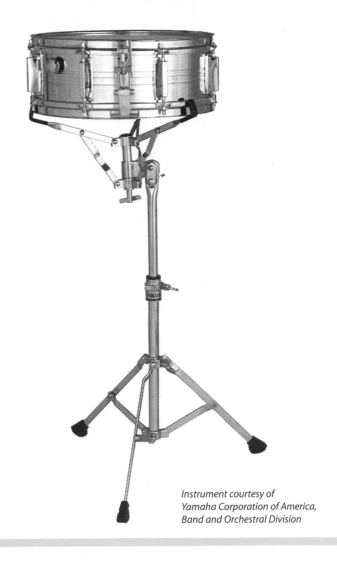

*Instrument courtesy of
Yamaha Corporation of America,
Band and Orchestral Division*

I. ROLL RUDIMENTS

A. SINGLE STROKE RUDIMENTS

1. Single Stroke Roll

2. Single Stroke Four

3. Single Stroke Seven

B. MULTIPLE BOUNCE ROLL RUDIMENTS

4. Multiple Bounce Roll

5. Triple Stroke Roll

*International Drum Rudiments courtesy of the Percussive Arts Society
Copyright © 1984*

SNARE DRUM INTERNATIONAL DRUM RUDIMENTS

C. DOUBLE STROKE OPEN ROLL RUDIMENTS

6. Double Stroke Open Roll

7. Five Stroke Roll

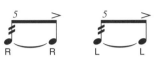

8. Six Stroke Roll

9. Seven Stroke Roll

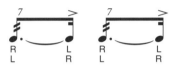

10. Nine Stroke Roll

11. Ten Stroke Roll

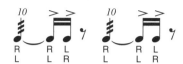

12. Eleven Stroke Roll

13. Thirteen Stroke Roll

14. Fifteen Stroke Roll

15. Seventeen Stroke Roll

II. DIDDLE RUDIMENTS

16. Single Paradiddle

17. Double Paradiddle

18. Triple Paradiddle

19. Single Paradiddle-Diddle

SNARE DRUM INTERNATIONAL DRUM RUDIMENTS

III. FLAM RUDIMENTS

20. Flam

21. Flam Accent

22. Flam Tap

23. Flamacue

24. Flam Paradiddle (Flamadiddle)

25. Single Flamed Mill

26. Flam Paradiddle-Diddle

27. Pataflafla

28. Swiss Army Triplet

29. Inverted Flam Tap

30. Flam Drag

SNARE DRUM INTERNATIONAL DRUM RUDIMENTS

IV. DRAG RUDIMENTS

31. Drag

36. Drag Paradiddle #1

32. Single Drag Tap

37. Drag Paradiddle #2

33. Double Drag Tap

38. Single Ratamacue

34. Lesson 25

39. Double Ratamacue

35. Single Dragadiddle

40. Triple Ratamacue

KEYBOARD PERCUSSION INSTRUMENTS

Each keyboard percussion instrument has a unique sound because of the materials used to create the instrument. Ranges may differ with some models of instruments.

Instrument Care Reminders

• Cover all percussion instruments when they are not being used.
• Put mallets away in a storage area. Keep the percussion section neat!
• Mallets are the only things which should be placed on your instrument. NEVER put or allow others to put objects on any percussion instrument.

BELLS (Orchestra Bells)

• Bars – metal alloy or steel
• Mallets – lexan (hard plastic), brass or hard rubber
• Range – 2 1/2 octaves
• Sounds 2 octaves higher than written

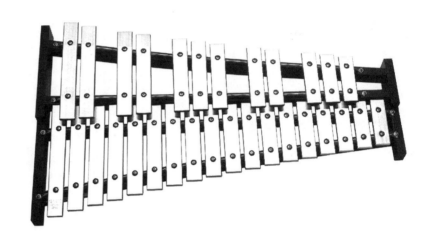

XYLOPHONE

• Bars – wooden or synthetic
• Mallets – hard rubber
• Range – 3 1/2 octaves
• Sounds 1 octave higher than written

MARIMBA

- Bars – wooden (wider than xylophone bars) Resonating tube located below each bar
- Mallets – soft to medium rubber or yarn covered
- Range – 4 1/3 octaves (reads bass and treble clefs)
- Sounding pitch is the same as written pitch

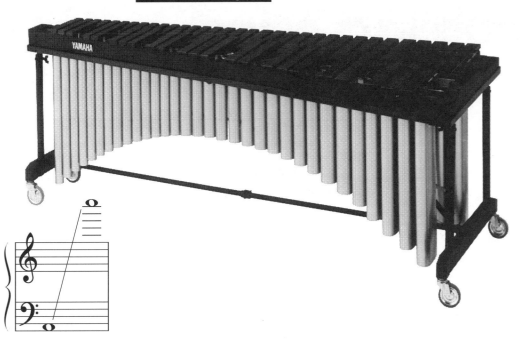

CHIMES

- Bars – metal tubes
- Mallets – plastic, rawhide or wooden
- Range – 1 1/2 octaves
- Sounding pitch is the same as written pitch

VIBRAPHONE

- Bars – metal alloy or aluminum Resonating tubes located below each bar Adjustable electric fans in each resonator create "vibrato" effect
- Mallets – yarn covered
- Range – 3 octaves
- Sounding pitch is the same as written pitch

Instruments and photos courtesy of Yamaha Corporation of America, Band and Orchestral Division

▚ REFERENCE INDEX

Definitions (pg.)

Book 1 Review

Composers

World Music

◢ REFERENCE INDEX FOR PERCUSSION

Definitions (pg.)

 PERCUSSION TIPS
**Additional Teaching Suggestions
By Will Rapp**

Percussion

1. TECHNIQUE TRAX
Strive for a consistent sound in this review of half, quarter, and eighth notes.

2. SHOO FLY
Remember to use multiple bounces based on eighth note hand motions.

3. THAILAND LULLABY
With yarn mallets on a suspended cymbal, use a rapid series of alternate strokes on the opposite edges of the cymbal (3 o'clock and 9 o'clock). Increase the speed of the roll to build an effective crescendo.

4. SHEPHERD'S HEY
Hold the tambourine steady in your left hand, at a slight, upward angle. Your right hand strikes the head of the instrument.

5. THE CRAWDAD SONG
Hold the open end of the cowbell away from you, and play on the front edge of the open end with a stick.

6. AMERICA/GOD SAVE THE QUEEN
Remember, striking the triangle on the side opposite the opening will produce a "fundamental" sound. Striking the bottom leg will produce a sound with more overtones (ringing). Listen to the band and decide which sound works best with the music. It's your choice.

7. WEARING OF THE GREEN
Follow the stickings carefully for the Flam Accent patterns. Handle-mounted sleigh bells can be played in one of two ways: holding the instrument parallel with the floor and shaking it in time, or tapping gently in time with the fist while holding the instrument perpendicular to the floor.

8. ROSES FROM THE SOUTH
Follow the dynamics in this piece carefully, paying special attention to the sound of the flams. To produce a timpani roll, rapidly alternate single strokes as smoothly as possible.

9. CRUISIN' THROUGH THE PARK
Careful attention to the accents is important. All accents in this piece are on the right hand.

10. TRUMPET VOLUNTARY – Duet
Emphasize listening to ensure the half notes on both bass drum and cymbals are played exactly together.

11. CHROMA-ZONE
This exercise is a good review of the double paradiddle. Note the accent placement of this rudiment.

Keyboard Percussion

1. TECHNIQUE TRAX
Encourage students to use Alternate Sticking, beginning with either the right or left hand.

2. SHOO FLY
You may need to remind keyboard percussion students that they do not play the second note of a tied note grouping.

3. THAILAND LULLABY
Alternate Sticking is suggested for this piece, beginning with the left hand; this will allow the right hand to lead in measure 6 for a more comfortable feeling.

4. SHEPHERD'S HEY
Alternate Sticking is suggested, beginning with the right hand. Additionally, students may wish to use Double Sticking on the repeated notes in the last measure.

5. THE CRAWDAD SONG
Doubling (Double Sticking) on the repeated eighth notes pitches is suggested for this piece. Measure 11 will work well using Alternate Sticking.

6. AMERICA/GOD SAVE THE QUEEN
Remind students to use long, slow strokes to enhance the legato feeling of this piece.

7. WEARING OF THE GREEN
Due to the starting note, students may find it easier to use Alternate Sticking leading with the left hand. This sticking is recommended for the beginning as well as the pick-up note into measure 3.

8. ROSES FROM THE SOUTH
Use long, slow strokes to match the legato quality of the woodwinds and brass instruments in this piece.

9. CRUISIN' THROUGH THE PARK
Alternate Sticking with a right hand lead is suggested for this exercise.

10. TRUMPET VOLUNTARY – Duet
The rolls in this piece are for Xylophone only. Bells should use long, slow strokes to produce legato half notes.

11. CHROMA-ZONE
Alternate Sticking with a right hand lead is suggested for this piece.

PERCUSSION TIPS (continued)

Percussion

12. BILLY BOY
This piece is a good example of how the sticking from a rudimental pattern can enhance musical phrasing. The character of the second beat is conditioned by how it is reached, in this case with a double sticking. When playing the wood block, remember that a hard rubber mallet or wooden xylophone mallet will produce a more characteristic sound than a drum stick.

13. TECHNIQUE TRAX
This exercise is a good review of both the eighth note and sixteenth note version of the triple paradiddle. The accent marks the beginning of each rudiment.

14. SALSA SIESTA – Duet
The Double Sticking suggested in this piece really helps to generate a nice Latin feel throughout. The placement of the accents is very important; have students remain relaxed on the entire pattern with emphasis on the accented notes. With all the attention to the sticking pattern and accent placement, it is important to give proper attention to the dynamic changes as well.

15. TREADING LIGHTLY
Remind students to use multiple bounces based on eighth note hand motions.

16. SMOOTH MOVE
This exercise features three different note lengths in the bass drum part, providing an excellent opportunity to develop the longer, slower strokes needed to achieve the longer note lengths.

17. SHIFTING GEARS
Review the various tambourine techniques which are based on dynamics:
- Soft light sounds – use one or two fingertips near the edge of the head.
- Medium loud sounds – use the tips of all fingers one-third of the way from the edge to the center.
- Loud sounds – knuckles on head, half-way between the edge and the center, use a motion similar to knocking on a door.

18. TALLIS CANON (Round)
To achieve a good sense of ensemble performance, all three percussion players must listen to hear how their parts fit together.

19. SIGHTREADING CHALLENGE
All performers must interpret the piano dynamic in such a way as to achieve a good balance between the snare drum, bass drum, triangle, and wood block.

20. TONE BUILDER
Students should take this opportunity to strive for a consistent sound with flams as they practice this exercise.

21. FLEXIBILITY STUDY
By now, students should be comfortable with various sticking systems such as: Right Hand Lead, Alternate, and Double Sticking. Encourage them to apply a different system each time they practice this exercise.

Keyboard Percussion

12. BILLY BOY
Students may wish to use a right hand lead on this exercise.

13. TECHNIQUE TRAX
Lift the mallet higher to produce an accented stroke.

14. SALSA SIESTA – Duet
Lift the mallets accordingly to produce the dynamic levels as marked in the music. If you have both Bells and Xylophone, have students split up; Bells play Part A, Xylophone plays Part B.

15. TREADING LIGHTLY
The rolls in this piece are for Xylophone only. Bells should use long, slow strokes to produce legato half notes.

16. SMOOTH MOVE
Remember to use long, slow strokes for the dotted half notes.

17. SHIFTING GEARS
The rolls in this piece are for Xylophone only. Bells should use very long, slow strokes to produce legato whole notes.

18. TALLIS CANON (Round)
Be aware of the constant change in dynamics throughout this exercise.

19. SIGHTREADING CHALLENGE
Use of longer, slower strokes on the dotted as well as tied notes will result in these notes sounding longer than quarter notes, which are played with a faster up-stroke.

20. TONE BUILDER
The rolls in this exercise are for Xylophone only. Bells should use long, slow strokes to produce legato half notes.

21. FLEXIBILITY STUDY
The rolls in this exercise are for Xylophone only. Bells should use long, slow strokes to produce legato half notes.

PERCUSSION TIPS (continued)

Percussion	Keyboard Percussion

22. TECHNIQUE TRAX
Note the paradiddle sticking without the traditional accent associated with this rudiment. This is an excellent exercise for developing stick control.

22. TECHNIQUE TRAX
Since this exercise follows the same melodic line played by the woodwinds, students should select a melodic sticking to fit the contour of the melodic line. Melodic sticking patterns are drawn from Alternate, Right Hand Lead, and Double Sticking systems.

23. CHORALE
On suspended cymbal, increase the speed of the roll to build an effective crescendo, and decrease the speed of the roll to shape an effective decrescendo. The same principle for controlling the roll can be applied to timpani.

23. CHORALE
Using long, slow strokes will help to match the legato sound played by the woodwinds and brass instruments.

24. GRANDFATHER'S CLOCK
Ask the temple blocks player to think of eighth notes in their mind in order not to rush the quarter note pulse.

24. GRANDFATHER'S CLOCK
Students may wish to use Double Sticking on the eighth notes that repeat in pitch throughout this piece. The roll is for Xylophone only.

25. GLOW WORM
Strive for a consistent sound when playing flam rudiments. Use a long multiple bounce roll on the fermata in the last measure.

25. GLOW WORM
Use a faster up-stroke to assist in achieving a lighter style throughout this exercise.

26. ALMA MATER
Remind the bass drum player that half notes require longer, slower strokes.

26. ALMA MATER
Use Legato Strokes to match the style of the woodwinds and brass in this piece.

27. LOCH LOMOND
Make sure students understand that the grace notes should be played slightly ahead of the beat so the principal note falls on the beat.

27. LOCH LOMOND
Students may wish to use doublings on repeated notes.

28. MOLLY MALONE
The strong pulse of the downbeat in triple meter is a perfect opportunity to use Flams. Notice how the flam tends to elongate the value of the quarter note, providing a contrast in length to the eighth notes that follow.

28. MOLLY MALONE
Students should select a melodic sticking to fit the contour of the melodic line.

29. RISE AND FALL
Pay attention to the height-of-rise, the distance that the stick moves away from the head, in order to correctly gauge the rate of crescendos and decrescendos.

29. RISE AND FALL
Students should select a melodic sticking to fit the contour of the melodic line.

30. NO COMPARISON
For the half note rolls, remember to use multiple bounces based on eighth note hand motions.

30. NO COMPARISON
Alternate Sticking with a right hand lead is suggested for this piece.

31. SIGHTREADING CHALLENGE
Have students double check their choice of sticking systems:
• If they use Right Hand Lead, then all Flams will be on the right hand.
• If they use Alternate Sticking, then the Flams will alternate hands.

31. SIGHTREADING CHALLENGE
While a key change can affect the choice of sticking, the sticking selected for the first half of this sightreading piece will also work for the second half.

32. RHYTHM RAP

32. RHYTHM RAP

33. A CUT ABOVE
Remind students to subdivide in order to avoid rushing the half notes.

33. A CUT ABOVE
Double Sticking is suggested for the repeated notes in this exercise.

 **PERCUSSION TIPS** (continued)

Percussion

34. TWO-FOUR YANKEE DOODLE
Keep the left hand low when moving from the last sixteenth note into the flam in measures 4 and 8. This technique will take some practice, but it is an important one to master.

35. CUT TIME YANKEE DOODLE
The same technique applies in the cut time version; the low positioning of the left hand is important for precise articulation of the flams.

36. MARIANNE
Remind students to use a short, precise wrist motion to shake the maracas. They should also focus on the speed of the eighth note to ensure that the quarter notes don't rush.

37. THE VICTORS
This is a good example of crash cymbal notation that asks for long note values (let ring) even though the note value selected is a short quarter note. Remind students to use a slower stroke to play these full value cymbal crashes.

38. ESSENTIAL CREATIVITY
Have students refer to the two examples of Yankee Doodle (34 and 35) if they are unsure of how to proceed with this creativity exercise. This type of rhythmic transposition is especially important for percussionists.

39. A – ROVING
Sudden changes in dynamics are best achieved through an adjustment in height-of-rise (the distance that the stick moves away from the head).

40. RHYTHM RAP

41. IN SYNC
Due to the nature of the snare drum sound, there is no difference in sound between the rhythms in measures 2 and 4 (or 6 and 7).

42. LA ROCA
The option to have one player play both the suspended cymbal and snare drum is provided as a subtle introduction to the Drum Set (introduced in exercise 54). Remind claves to cup the left hand to form a resonating chamber. Hold the lower pitched clave in the left hand. Use the clave in the right hand to strike the center of the left clave.

43. ESSENTIAL ELEMENTS QUIZ– YOU'RE A GRAND OLD FLAG
In addition to the flams and multiple bounce rolls used in this piece, attention must be also directed toward the accent placement and the dynamic markings.

Keyboard Percussion

34. TWO-FOUR YANKEE DOODLE
Alternate Sticking with a left hand lead is suggested for this piece.

35. CUT TIME YANKEE DOODLE
Alternate Sticking with a left hand lead is suggested for this piece.

36. MARIANNE
Bells should use long, slow strokes on notes that are marked as rolls on Xylophone.

37. THE VICTORS
Students should select a melodic sticking to fit the contour of the melodic line.

38. ESSENTIAL CREATIVITY

39. A – ROVING
Use a faster up-stroke on the eighth notes in this exercise to achieve the proper spacing.

40. RHYTHM RAP

41. IN SYNC
You may wish to suggest the use of a Natural Sticking for this syncopation exercise. Beginning with the right hand, use Alternate Sticking on each eighth note. In the syncopated measures (or measures with rests) skip over the sticking that would occur at that point and move to the other hand. Natural Sticking in measures 2, 4, 6, and 7 would be R L L.

42. LA ROCA
Alternate Sticking with a left hand lead is suggested for this piece.

43. ESSENTIAL ELEMENTS QUIZ – YOU'RE A GRAND OLD FLAG
Emphasize the accents by lifting the mallet higher on the accented notes.

 **PERCUSSION TIPS** (continued)

Percussion

44. KEY MOMENT
The smaller muscles in the fingers, hands, and wrists function with more control once the larger muscles in the forearms are loose and relaxed. The sticking pattern presented in this exercise is excellent as a daily warm-up.

45. THE MINSTREL BOY
Notice how the faster rhythms of the percussion part support the slower rhythms of the melodic line. Encourage students to listen to the melody as they play the snare drum part.

46. CLOSE CALL
This is another example of a faster rhythm in percussion supporting the slower rhythm of the melodic line. Remember, a matched pair of bass drum mallets is needed for the roll in the last measure.

47. VICTORY MARCH
When playing crash cymbals, use short, glancing strokes for eighth notes, and the same motion but slower for quarter notes. For half notes, the stroke should be slower still.

48. WINNING STREAK
The same crash cymbal techniques apply to this exercise as well. Have students focus on the sound quality of the cymbals, not the dynamic level.

49. SIGHTREADING CHALLENGE
The Bass Drum player should use care to group the eighth note rest as part of the syncopated figure that precedes it.

50. RHYTHM RAP

51. SIXTEENTH NOTE FANFARE
Percussionists should listen carefully not to get ahead of the winds and brass, who are playing sixteenth notes for the first time.

52. MOVING ALONG
The percussion parts are written to support the winds and brass in the early stages of playing sixteenth notes. Care should be taken not to rush these rhythms.

53. BACK AND FORTH – Duet
Percussionists should listen carefully in order to balance the sounds of the Snare Drum with the Tom-Tom part. The Bass Drum needs to listen to both Snare Drum and Tom-Tom parts to achieve good ensemble precision.

54. COMIN' ROUND THE MOUNTAIN VARIATIONS
While the Hi-Hat is also an important part of the Drum Set, it has been omitted at first in order to focus on the three-way coordination required of the two hands and the bass drum foot pedal. If you have a student who already has some drum set experience, the Hi-Hat (played with the left foot) may be added on beats 2 and 4.

Keyboard Percussion

44. KEY MOMENT
Students should use Alternate Sticking with a left hand lead for this exercise. This will avoid unnecessary crossing in the hands on the arpeggio at the end.

45. THE MINSTREL BOY
Alternate Sticking with a left hand lead is suggested for this piece.

46. CLOSE CALL
Students should select a melodic sticking to fit the contour of the melodic line.

47. VICTORY MARCH
Emphasize the accents by lifting the mallet higher on the accented notes.

48. WINNING STREAK
Emphasize the accents by lifting the mallet higher on the accented notes.

49. SIGHTREADING CHALLENGE
Students should select a melodic sticking to fit the contour of the melodic line.

50. RHYTHM RAP

51. SIXTEENTH NOTE FANFARE
Keyboard percussionists should listen carefully not to get ahead of the woodwinds and brass, who are playing sixteenth notes for the first time. Alternate Sticking with a right hand lead is suggested for this piece.

52. MOVING ALONG
Alternate Sticking with a left hand lead is suggested for this exercise.

53. BACK AND FORTH – Duet
If you have both Bells and Xylophone, have students split up; Bells play Part A, Xylophone plays Part B.

54. COMIN' ROUND THE MOUNTAIN VARIATIONS
Students should select a melodic sticking to fit the contour of the melodic line.

PERCUSSION TIPS (continued)

| Percussion | Keyboard Percussion |

Percussion

55. ESSENTIAL ELEMENTS QUIZ
Students may be more comfortable using the Right Hand Lead system for this quiz, which will allow the flams to be played with the right hand.

56. WARM-UP CHORALE
Remind students playing suspended cymbal to increase the speed of the roll to build an effective crescendo, and decrease the speed of the roll to shape an effective decrescendo.

57. THE THUNDERER – Band Arrangement
The multiple bounce quarter notes should be played with four multiple bounce sixteenth note hand motions connected together as smoothly as possible. Beginning in measure 5, subdivide each multiple bounce eighth note into two equal sixteenth note multiple bounce hand motions and connect them as smoothly as possible.

58. HILL AND GULLY RIDER – Band Arrangement
To achieve a good sense of ensemble performance, the four percussion parts should listen to how they all fit together. The traditional "clave" rhythm is used here, supported by a bass drum part that fits into this rhythm. Maracas should use short, precise strokes to match the sound of the bongos.

59. SHENANDOAH – Band Arrangement
This is a good exercise of percussion writing that supports the wind score without being too active. Students should focus on the quality of their sound as well as how the dynamics highlight the overall expression of the piece.

60. LAS MAÑANITAS – Band Arrangement
Students should be aware of the quality of sound they are producing on the four different instruments. Proper balance is achieved once each percussionist is able to hear all the parts at the same time.

61. RONDEAU – Band Arrangement
When playing drags, the grace notes should be played slightly ahead of the beat so that the the principal note falls on the beat. Use long, slow strokes to play half notes on timpani for their full value.

62. ROCK.COM – Encore Band Arrangement
If you have a student who already has some drum set experience, the Hi-Hat (played with the left foot) may be added on beats 2 and 4. If a Drum Set is not available or you wish to use the entire percussion section instead, the parts can be assigned to three different players. The cowbell is the real "time-keeper" of this piece.

63. RHYTHM RAP

64. SIXTEENTH VARIATIONS
Percussionists should listen carefully to the winds and brass who are playing the [♪♫] rhythm for the first time.

Keyboard Percussion

55. ESSENTIAL ELEMENTS QUIZ
Students should select a melodic sticking to fit the contour of the melodic line.

56. WARM-UP CHORALE
Use Legato Strokes to match the style of the woodwinds and brass in this chorale.

57. THE THUNDERER – Band Arrangement
Emphasize all accents and select a melodic sticking to fit the contour of the melodic line.

58. HILL AND GULLY RIDER – Band Arrangement
The Natural Sticking pattern of R L L will work well in the syncopated measures containing repeated notes.

59. SHENANDOAH – Band Arrangement
Remember to use long, slow strokes on all note values longer than a quarter note to achieve a flowing sound.

60. LAS MAÑANITAS – Band Arrangement
The style of this piece is best expressed by using lighter strokes with a faster up-stroke on the eighth notes to enhance the character of the music.

61. RONDEAU – Band Arrangement
Alternate Sticking with a right hand lead is suggested for this exercise.

62. ROCK.COM – Encore Band Arrangement
Double Sticking is suggested for all repeated notes.

63. RHYTHM RAP

64. SIXTEENTH VARIATIONS
Alternate Sticking with a right hand lead is suggested for this exercise.

PERCUSSION TIPS (continued)

Percussion

65. SEA CHANTEY
Two entirely different techniques are used to play the same rhythm on Snare Drum and Tambourine, so it is important for the players to listen to each other. Don't be concerned if the tambourine player is not able to make the crescendo at first. Students should focus their attention on learning the Knee to Fist Technique.

66. AMERICAN FANFARE
The percussion parts are written to support the wind and brass parts. Care should be taken not to rush these rhythms.

67. SCALE STUDY
This Flam Rudiment Review provides an opportunity for students to also review stick position guidelines for flam taps. After you play a flam, play a tap, always with the low hand. This will keep the hands correctly positioned for the rest of the measure. When moving to the Flam Paradiddle in measure 3, use the high hand to play the stroke after the flam.

68. BILL BAILEY
If you have a student who already has some drum set experience, the Hi-Hat (played with the left foot) may be added on beats 2 and 4 in place of the Crash Cymbal chokes (Hi-Hat style).

69. RHYTHM RAP

70. RHYTHM ETUDE
Percussionists should listen carefully to the winds and brass who are playing the [♪♫♩] rhythm for the first time.

71. BATTLE STATIONS
Students playing Snare Drum and Concert Tom-Toms need to listen to each other to ensure that these unison rhythms are played with good ensemble precision. The larger Concert Tom-Toms played with felt mallets tend to respond more slowly than a Snare Drum played with sticks.

72. ENGLISH DANCE
Proper attention to dynamics is necessary to achieve good ensemble balance between the four separate percussion parts. Students should focus attention on the last note of the piece to make sure that all sounds release together.

73. BIG ROCK CANDY MOUNTAIN
Emphasize the accents in the fourth measure of each phrase (first ending, second ending, and measure 10) to mark the syncopated figures in this piece. The technique for playing sixteenth notes with an accent on the tambourine is similar to the technique used to play this instrument in a pop music setting.

74. ESSENTIAL ELEMENTS QUIZ
You have the option of assigning separate players for the triangle and wood block parts, or asking one player to cover them both. Remember the interpretation for drags; the grace notes should be played slightly ahead of the beat so that the principal note falls on the beat.

Keyboard Percussion

65. SEA CHANTEY
Students may wish to experiment with both Alternate Sticking and Double Sticking systems in this exercise.

66. AMERICAN FANFARE
Students may wish to experiment with both a right hand lead and a left hand lead as they apply Alternate Sticking to this piece.

67. SCALE STUDY
Alternate Sticking with a left hand lead is suggested for this scale study.

68. BILL BAILEY
Attention to accent placement as well as duration of the rolls is important in this exercise.

69. RHYTHM RAP

70. RHYTHM ETUDE
Alternate Sticking with a right hand lead is suggested for this exercise.

71. BATTLE STATIONS
This is a good exercise to practice Double Sticking. Students may begin with either a double right or a double left.

72. ENGLISH DANCE
Students should be aware of the three different dynamic levels required to perform this piece and adjust the height of the mallets accordingly.

73. BIG ROCK CANDY MOUNTAIN
Double Sticking is suggested for all repeated notes. The four sixteenth notes in measure 7 should be played with Alternate Sticking.

74. ESSENTIAL ELEMENTS QUIZ
Alternate Sticking with a left hand lead is suggested for this quiz. Use Double Sticking on repeated sixteenth note patterns.

 **PERCUSSION TIPS** (continued)

<table>
<tr><td>

Percussion

75. SIMPLE SONG – Duet
Keep the spacing between the grace note and the principal note of the flams consistent even when moving through a rallentando measure.

76. LINE DANCE
Remind students playing the wood block that a hard rubber mallet or wooden xylophone mallet will produce a more characteristic sound than a drum stick. This part can be played with only one mallet.

77. TECHNIQUE TRAX
Students have the option here of using either Alternate Sticking or applying rudiments such as Flam Paradiddle (measures 1, 3, and 5) and Flamacue (measure 2, 4, and 8).

78. THE GALWAY PIPER
Review the technique for medium loud sounds on the Tambourine: use the tips of fingers one-third of the way from the edge to the center of the head.

79. MANHATTAN BEACH MARCH
While the Bass Drum plays half notes for most of the piece, the Crash Cymbals play alternating measures of half notes and whole notes. While students tend to move the cymbals faster on an accented note, remind them to use longer, slower strokes on the whole notes.

80. SIGHTREADING CHALLENGE
Notice that there are three different note lengths in the Bass Drum part. Students should accommodate these different note lengths with the appropriate length of stroke.

81. RHYTHM RAP

82. MARCHING ALONG
Percussionists should listen carefully to the winds and brass who are playing the [♩♫] rhythm for the first time. Care should be taken to not rush this new rhythm.

83. FANFARE FOR BAND – Trio
Encourage students to continue using the counting system from the previous exercise to ensure accurate rhythmic interpretation of the [♩♫] rhythm in measures 3 and 4. Percussionists can provide an excellent model for the winds and brass because the rhythms are identical to the other parts of the trio.

84. O TANNENBAUM
The Timpani provide excellent support for this well-known German Carol while the Triangle and Suspended Cymbal provide additional tone color. Use long, slow strokes when playing the Timpani part for this piece.

85. S'VIVON
Review the Tambourine Shake: Hold the Tambourine with either the left or right hand and stop the shake on the release (tied) note with the fingertips of the opposite hand. It will take some practice to incorporate the shake into the rhythm of the part.

</td><td>

Keyboard Percussion

75. SIMPLE SONG – Duet
If you have both Bells and Xylophone, have students split up; Bells play Part A, Xylophone plays Part B.

76. LINE DANCE
This is a good exercise to practice Double Sticking on the sixteenth notes with repeated pitches.

77. TECHNIQUE TRAX
Alternate Sticking with a right hand lead is suggested for this exercise.

78. THE GALWAY PIPER
Alternate Sticking with a left hand lead is suggested for this exercise.

79. MANHATTAN BEACH MARCH
Use long, slow strokes on the tied notes to achieve full note value throughout this piece.

80. SIGHTREADING CHALLENGE
Students should select a melodic sticking to fit the contour of the melodic line.

81. RHYTHM RAP

82. MARCHING ALONG
Alternate Sticking with a right hand lead is suggested for this exercise.

83. FANFARE FOR BAND – Trio
If you do not have three keyboard percussion instruments, you may wish to consider playing Part C one octave lower on the Xylophone in order that two students might share the same instrument.

84. O TANNENBAUM
Alternate Sticking with a left hand lead is suggested for this exercise, especially to maintain the continuity of the [♩♫] rhythms.

85. S'VIVON
Students may wish to use Double Sticking on the repeated eighth note pitches throughout this exercise.

</td></tr>
</table>

 **PERCUSSION TIPS** (continued)

Percussion

86. GOOD KING WENCESLAS
Remind students that handle-mounted sleigh bells can be played in one of two ways; holding the instrument parallel with the floor and shaking it in time, or tapping gently in time with the fist while holding the instrument perpendicular to the floor.

87. TONE BUILDER
Now that students have accomplished multiple bounce rolls, it is time to begin the study of open (measured) rolls. Double Bounces are first applied to sixteenth note patterns to serve as an orientation to the technique of moving the wrist once to produce two notes.

88. FLEXIBILITY STUDY
Notice how the rhythm in the first half of the measure sets the correct speed for the hand motions needed to play the five-stroke open rolls that follow. When students first hear open rolls, they imagine that faster hand motions are needed. Actually, the hand motions are the same speed as sixteenth notes, but each motion has two bounces.

89. TECHNIQUE TRAX
Once again, the rhythm in measure one sets the correct speed for the hand motions to play the nine-stroke open roll that follows. It is extremely important that students understand the relationship between the speed of the hand motions and the sound of the open roll.

90. CHORALE
Students should listen to how the Suspended Cymbal part supports both the crescendos and decrescendos in the wind and brass parts.

91. TOREADOR SONG (from CARMEN)
In order to foster success with playing open rolls, it is important to select a performance tempo that supports the development of double bounces. Begin with a tempo of approximately ($\quarternote = 88$) and work up to ($\quarternote = 98$).

92. LA CUMPARSITA
Rather than simply concentrating on their own parts, students should be encouraged to listen to the dialog between the Snare Drum/Bass Drum part and the Timbales part.

93. THE YELLOW ROSE OF TEXAS
Remind students that the longer the note, the slower the stroke on the cymbals. Since the entire piece is marked at *mf*, the focus can be on the quality of the sound production.

94. SCALE STUDY
Remember to use four sixteenth note hand motions to correctly play the nine-stroke open rolls in measures 1, 3, and 4. The five-stroke open rolls in the last half of the piece are preceded by the number of sixteenth hand motions that will correctly set the speed of the hands.

Keyboard Percussion

86. GOOD KING WENCESLAS
Alternate Sticking with a left hand lead is suggested with a Doubling on repeated half notes at the end of each phrase.

87. TONE BUILDER
Use Legato Strokes to match the sound of the woodwinds and brass in this exercise.

88. FLEXIBILITY STUDY
Play each two-measure phrase with Alternate Sticking, beginning with the right hand.

89. TECHNIQUE TRAX
Alternate Sticking with a right hand lead is suggested for this exercise.

90. CHORALE
Use Legato Strokes to match the sound of the woodwinds and brass in this chorale.

91. TOREADOR SONG (from CARMEN)
Both accent placement and dynamic contrast are important in this piece. Students should select a melodic sticking to fit the contour of the melodic line.

92. LA CUMPARSITA
Students should carefully select a melodic sticking to fit the contour of this melodic line containing chromatic notes.

93. THE YELLOW ROSE OF TEXAS
Students should select a melodic sticking to fit the contour of the melodic line.

94. SCALE STUDY
Begin this scale study with a left hand lead. In the last half of the study, Doublings can be used on the repeated sixteenth note pitches.

PERCUSSION TIPS (continued)

Percussion	Keyboard Percussion

Percussion

95. ADVANCE AUSTRALIA FAIR
Keep the spacing between the grace notes and the principal note of the drags consistent even when moving through the two-measure *rit.* near the end of the piece.

96. ESSENTIAL CREATIVITY

97. AMERICAN PATROL
Using a Flamacue in measures 1, 2, 9, and 10 really helps to emphasize the syncopation.

98. ARIA (from MARRIAGE OF FIGARO)
Students should focus on the quality of their sound as they provide a light, yet effective accompaniment to this aria excerpt.

99. THE STARS AND STRIPES FOREVER
Students playing Bass Drum and Crash Cymbals should be positioned close to one another in order to play together with good ensemble precision. You may wish to tell students that historically, one person often played the bass drum with attached cymbals. Therefore, while being two players, they must sound like "one".

100. SIGHTREADING CHALLENGE
Remember to use four sixteenth note hand motions to correctly play the nine-stroke open rolls in measures 1, 2, 5, 6, and 8.

101. RHYTHM RAP

102. LAZY DAY
This is an excellent example of two ancient drum rudiments: Flam Accent No. 1 (measure 1) and Flam Accent No. 2 (measure 3). They have since been replaced by the more modern interpretation of Flam Accent (see page 47).

103. ROW YOUR BOAT
Although the multiple bounces are notated individually, the resulting sound should be a smooth connection between the first multiple bounce and the release.

104. JOLLY GOOD FELLOW
If students begin this exercise with the right hand (pick-up on beat 6), then all multiple bounce rolls will begin with the right hand as well.

105. CHANSON
Students should focus on the consistency of flams throughout this exercise.

106. ESSENTIAL ELEMENTS QUIZ – WHEN JOHNNY COMES MARCHING HOME
Bass Drum and Crash Cymbals should use longer, slower strokes on the dotted half notes in this piece. Remember the interpretation for drags; the grace notes should be played slightly ahead of the beat so that the principal note falls on the beat.

Keyboard Percussion

95. ADVANCE AUSTRALIA FAIR
Pay strict attention to the release of each of the rolled notes in order to develop consistency with this technique.

96. ESSENTIAL CREATIVITY

97. AMERICAN PATROL
Students should select a melodic sticking according to the contour of the melodic line for this exercise.

98. ARIA (from MARRIAGE OF FIGARO)
This excerpt provides an excellent opportunity to work on the technique of using Double Sticking on repeated notes of different rhythms in order to achieve a phrasing concept. Experiment with using double right hand sticking on the [♪♪] rhythms in this exercise.

99. THE STARS AND STRIPES FOREVER
Pay strict attention to the release of each of the rolled notes in order to develop consistency with this technique.

100. SIGHTREADING CHALLENGE
The same technique of applying Doublings to repeated notes of different rhythm (exercise 98) can be used in this piece as well.

101. RHYTHM RAP

102. LAZY DAY
This exercise works well with either left hand or right hand lead.

103. ROW YOUR BOAT
Alternate Sticking with a right hand lead is suggested for this exercise.

104. JOLLY GOOD FELLOW
Alternate Sticking with a left hand lead is suggested for this exercise.

105. CHANSON
Although there is not much of a dynamic change in this piece, students should be aware of the crescendo as they move from measure 4 to 5.

106. ESSENTIAL ELEMENTS QUIZ – WHEN JOHNNY COMES MARCHING HOME
It is important not to rush to the last beat of the measure after the release of the rolled notes. In each case, the last note of the rolled measure will be on the right hand, so practice lifting the right mallet after the release of the roll to prepare for the sixth beat of the measure.

PERCUSSION TIPS (continued)

Percussion

107. CHROMATIC SCALE
Make sure students understand that the change from the sixteenth notes to the seventeen-stroke open roll involves a change of technique (from stroking to double bounce), not a change of speed in the hand motions.

108. TECHNIQUE TRAX
If you have a student who already has some drum set experience, the Hi-Hat (played with the left foot) may be added on beats 2 and 4.

109. HABAÑERA (from CARMEN)
The head of the Tambourine cannot be too smooth for a thumb roll to work properly. Some beeswax or bow rosin applied to the edge of the head will help the thumb to get a better "grip."

110. CHROMATIC CRESCENDO
The application of a crescendo to a multiple bounce roll takes some practice. Concentrate on a smooth multiple bounce sound and allow the crescendo to build through the single strokes. Watch the *rall.* at the end.

111. TURKISH MARCH (from THE RUINS OF ATHENS)
Use long, slow strokes to play the half notes in the Bass Drum and Triangle parts. Remember the interpretation for drags; the grace notes should be played slightly ahead of the beat so that the principal note falls on the beat.

112. THE OVERLANDER
Emphasize the accents throughout this piece by making sure that the dynamic level is a *mp* throughout. The Crash Cymbal note in the last measure should be played with a long, slow stroke.

113. STACCATO STUDY
Double sticking patterns must be played precisely in order to support the staccato articulations in the wind and brass parts. Remind students that articulation is the pronunciation of musical sound. As two entirely different techniques are used to play the same rhythm on Snare Drum and Tambourine, it is important for the players to listen to each other.

114. YANKEE DOODLE DANDY
Notice the ensemble accents in measures 13 and 29. Snare Drum, Bass Drum, and Crash Cymbals should emphasize this accent to effectively mark this important syncopation.

115. SIGHTREADING CHALLENGE
Use the technique of connecting eighth note multiple bounce hand motions (see exercises 103 and 104) to achieve the dotted half note roll after the second ending.

116. RHYTHM RAP

117. THREE TO GET READY
The Snare Drum rhythms are the same as in the wind and brass parts; percussionists should listen to the band for ensemble precision.

Keyboard Percussion

107. CHROMATIC SCALE
Use long, slow strokes to play this chromatic scale.

108. TECHNIQUE TRAX
Students should focus on the sticking patterns that are least comfortable during individual practice in order to improve overall technique.

109. HABAÑERA (from CARMEN)
Developing the technique to release the roll at the end of the phrase in time to quickly move the right mallet to high C will take some practice. Always think of the motion for a leap as an arc, with continuous flow from the low note to the high note.

110. CHROMATIC CRESCENDO
Alternate the chromatic notes and Double the repeated notes in this exercise.

111. TURKISH MARCH (from THE RUINS OF ATHENS)
Doubling the repeated eighth note pitches in measures 2 and 6 will give the right hand more time to make the octave leap.

112. THE OVERLANDER
Use longer, slower strokes for the longer note values of this exercise.

113. STACCATO STUDY
Use a left hand lead and Double the repeated sixteenth note figures in this study.

114. YANKEE DOODLE DANDY
It is important to release the half note rolls in enough time to stay in tempo. Listen for consistency in the release of the half note rolls tied to quarter notes.

115. SIGHTREADING CHALLENGE
Students should select a melodic sticking according to the contour of the melodic line.

116. RHYTHM RAP

117. THREE TO GET READY
Alternate Sticking is suggested for this exercise.

PERCUSSION TIPS (continued)

Percussion

118. TRIPLET STUDY
Use the same technique for multiple bounce rolls in triplets as was used in 6/8 meter.

119. MARCH (from THE NUTCRACKER) – Duet
Since the first phrase of music has a triplet feel, you may wish to encourage students to use the triplet multiple bounce approach (from exercise 118) to play the half note multiple bounce rolls in measures 2 and 4. Remind students to shift their counting system to sixteenth notes in order to correctly interpret the second phrase.

120. ESSENTIAL ELEMENTS QUIZ - THEME FROM FAUST
Here as well, use of the triplet multiple bounce approach to play the half note and quarter note multiple bounce rolls is a desirable interpretation.

121. SCALE STUDY
This exercise allows an excellent opportunity to develop the triplet multiple bounce approach, a technique which allows multiple bounce rolls to be played with a "seamless" sound when the tempo does not suit a duple multiple bounce approach.

122. OVER THE RIVER AND THROUGH THE WOODS
The same multiple bounce approach used in the previous exercise can be applied to this 6/8 piece.

123. RHYTHM RAP

124. ON THE MOVE
This pattern can be doubled on the Drum Set if you have a student with some experience.

125. HIGHER GROUND
This piece has been written in a through-composed style to match the wind and brass parts. In addition to correct rhythms, adding to the complexity of the part are the placement of accents, flams, drags, and multiple bounce rolls. Students having difficulty should work for correct rhythms first, then add accents, and finally add the embellishments (one at a time if necessary).

126. ESSENTIAL ELEMENTS QUIZ
Students having difficulty with this quiz should use the practice method described in the previous exercise.

127. THE MARINES' HYMN
Cut time can initially pose a problem to percussionists because they have to transpose the notation of open rolls (in their mind). In 4/4, the half note open roll has seventeen strokes; in cut time it only has nine.

128. D.S. MARCH
This piece, written in 2/4, allows students to see the five-, nine-, and seventeen-stroke open rolls in the original notation in which they were learned.

Keyboard Percussion

118. TRIPLET STUDY
Due to the accidentals in this exercise, students may be more comfortable using Alternate Sticking with a left hand lead.

119. MARCH (from THE NUTCRACKER) – Duet
If you have both Bells and Xylophone, have students split up; Bells play Part A, Xylophone plays Part B.

120. ESSENTIAL ELEMENTS QUIZ – THEME FROM FAUST
Due to the accidentals in this piece, students may be more comfortable using Alternate Sticking with a left hand lead.

121. SCALE STUDY
Use Legato Strokes on the half notes to match the sound of the woodwinds and brass.

122. OVER THE RIVER AND THROUGH THE WOODS
Using Natural Sticking with a left hand lead will produce a L L R R sticking in the measure 2. This will result in phrasing that has a nice flow.

123. RHYTHM RAP

124. ON THE MOVE
Students have the choice here of using a strict Alternate Sticking or using doublings for the repeated figures of two sixteenth notes.

125. HIGHER GROUND
This is an excellent exercise in which to use the Right Hand Lead system of sticking. In this system, the right hand plays on every quarter note pulse of the measure.

126. ESSENTIAL ELEMENTS QUIZ
By now, keyboard percussion students should be developing sticking systems that provide effective musical results. Allow students to use the sticking system that feels most comfortable to them for this quiz.

127. THE MARINES' HYMN
Students should select a melodic sticking according to the contour of the melodic line.

128. D.S. MARCH
Remind students that the most effective way to emphasize the accents is to lift the mallet a little higher. This height-of-rise approach is more desirable than striking the bar harder.

 **PERCUSSION TIPS** (continued)

Percussion	**Keyboard Percussion**

129. CAN-CAN
Keep the spacing between the grace note and the principal note of the flams consistent even when moving through the accelerando measures. Use long, slow strokes to play the quarter notes in the Timpani part. In the last measure, the accents should be played by lifting the stroke (and the sound) out of the head.

129. CAN-CAN
For the *accel.*, using a light stroke with a faster up-stroke will be more effective.

130. TARANTELLA
As two entirely different techniques are used to play the same rhythm on Snare Drum and Tambourine, it is important for the players to listen to each other.

130. TARANTELLA
Using Natural Sticking with a left hand lead will produce a L L R R L L sticking at the beginning of the piece. This sticking pattern also helps to define the form of this dance.

131. EMPEROR WALTZ
Remind students to thinks of flams as embellishments of length (not as accents), especially in 3/4 where there is an emphasis on the first beat of each measure.

131. EMPEROR WALTZ
Care should be taken to release the rolled notes in enough time to maintain the tempo of the exercise.

132. ENGLISH DANCE – Duet
Students should understand that the use of Natural Sticking in 6/8 dance music provides forward movement in the phrasing more effectively than with Alternate Sticking.

132. ENGLISH DANCE – Duet
If you have both Bells and Xylophone, have students split up; Bells play Part A, Xylophone plays Part B.

133. ESSENTIAL ELEMENTS QUIZ – BRITISH GRENADIERS
Students should focus on producing a consistent sound with the open rolls. In the Timpani part, use long, slow strokes when playing the quarter notes.

133. ESSENTIAL ELEMENTS QUIZ – BRITISH GRENADIERS
Alternate Sticking with a left hand lead is suggested for this exercise.

134. NASSAU BOUND
Congas should concentrate on producing a nice open tone on all notes, using the introductory technique provided in the shaded box. (Students will eventually learn other techniques for accents.) The rim shot (with snares off) is intended to be more of a subtle effect. By using a double left sticking on the last two eighth notes in measure 1, all rim shots will then be played with the right hand.

134. NASSAU BOUND
Use of Natural Sticking will encourage good phrasing during the syncopated figures in this exercise.

135. UNFINISHED SYMPHONY THEME
At this consistent dynamic level *mp*, students can concentrate on producing consistent sounds with flams, drags, and multiple bounce rolls. The character of this piece is such that using sixteenth note hand motions for the multiple bounce rolls will provide a smooth, connected sound.

135. UNFINISHED SYMPHONY THEME
Students should select a melodic sticking according to the contour of the melodic line.

136. RHYTHM STUDY
These rhythms are identical to those of the wind and brass parts, but with the addition of flams, flam taps, and drags. Care should be taken not to let the embellishments alter the precision of the rhythms.

136. RHYTHM STUDY
Alternate Sticking with a right hand lead is suggested for this rhythm study.

137. COUNTRY GARDENS
The wood block is the real "time-keeper" of this piece. All three percussion instruments must be aware of making dynamic changes and observing the *rall.* as an ensemble.

137. COUNTRY GARDENS
Use a light stroke with a faster up-stroke in order to achieve the proper phrasing and character for this well-known English folk song.

138. JOSHUA
Emphasize all accents and make sure that the doublings are individually stroked; these are not double bounces.

138. JOSHUA
Use of Natural Sticking will provide a good phrasing concept for the syncopated figures in this piece.

PERCUSSION TIPS (continued)

Percussion	**Keyboard Percussion**

139. LISTEN TO THE MOCKINGBIRD
The Wood Block part will require two mallets for accurate performance. Hard rubber mallets or wooden xylophone mallets will produce a more characteristic sound than Snare Drum sticks.

139. LISTEN TO THE MOCKINGBIRD
Alternate Sticking with a right hand lead is suggested for this exercise.

140. ANCHORS AWEIGH
Alternate Sticking is recommended for proper articulation of the sixteenth note triplet rhythms.

140. ANCHORS AWEIGH
Students should select a melodic sticking according to the contour of the melodic line.

141. GREENSLEEVES
Striking the side of the Triangle opposite the open end will produce a "fundamental" sound. Striking the bottom leg will produce a sound with more overtones (ringing). Listen to the band and decide which sound works best with the music. It's your choice

141. GREENSLEEVES
Students should select a melodic sticking according to the contour of the melodic line.

142. THE LONG CLIMB
Students need to maintain a consistent sixteenth note speed regardless of the changes in paradiddle sticking.

142. THE LONG CLIMB
Alternate Sticking with either a left hand or right hand lead will work for this exercise.

143. THE BLUE BELLS OF SCOTLAND
Alternate Sticking is recommended for proper articulation of the sixteenth note triplet rhythms.

143. THE BLUE BELLS OF SCOTLAND
Alternate Sticking with a left hand lead is suggested for this piece.

144. NATURAL MINOR SCALE
Continue to use Alternate Sticking for proper articulation of these sixteenth note triplet rhythms.

144. NATURAL MINOR SCALE
Use Legato Strokes to match the sound of the woodwinds and brass. Alternate Sticking with a left hand lead is suggested.

145. FINALE FROM "NEW WORLD SYMPHONY"
This exercise combines the two previous forms of sixteenth note triplet rhythms. Using Alternate Sticking, the sixteenth note triplet rhythms beginning on the beat will be played with the right hand leading, and those beginning on the up-beat will be played with the left hand leading.

145. FINALE FROM "NEW WORLD SYMPHONY"
It is important to lift the mallet on the accented strokes, but this lift must include a slow up-stroke to achieve full note value.

146. HARMONIC MINOR SCALE
Students may inadvertently play accents on the first and fourth notes of this sixteenth note triplet rhythm. Encourage them to think of moving directly from beat 1 to beat 2 (and beat 3 to beat 4) by playing seven notes without accenting.

146. HARMONIC MINOR SCALE
Use Legato Strokes to match the sound of the woodwinds and brass. Alternate Sticking with a left hand lead is suggested.

147. HUNGARIAN DANCE NO. 5
Due to the nature of the knee-to-fist Tambourine part played against the Snare Drum Flams, the players must listen to each other carefully to ensure proper ensemble¡e precision.

147. HUNGARIAN DANCE NO. 5
Students should select a melodic sticking according to the contour of the melodic line.

148. POMP AND CIRCUMSTANCE
Strive for even sixteenth note triplet patterns containing no accents, especially when two sets of these patterns are played in close succession.

148. POMP AND CIRCUMSTANCE
Care should be taken to release the rolled notes in enough time to maintain the tempo of the exercise.

149. SIMPLE GIFTS – Band Arrangement
Remind percussionists to pay strict attention to all dynamic markings throughout this piece in order to achieve an effective performance.

149. SIMPLE GIFTS – Band Arrangement
Use long, slow strokes on half notes. This is especially important when playing double stopped whole notes.

PERCUSSION TIPS (continued)

| Percussion | Keyboard Percussion |

Percussion

150. SEMPER FIDELIS – Band Arrangement
Open measured rolls in 6/8 take some practice in order to flow smoothly. It is important that the tempo selected is within the "window" which allows the student to effectively employ the technique of playing eighth notes, then applying a double bounce to each hand motion.

151. DANNY BOY – Band Arrangement
Students may wish to play the multiple bounce rolls in this piece by using eighth note triplet hand motions for the rolls, thus keeping the hands in exact rhythm with the rhythm that precedes each roll.

152. TAKE ME OUT TO THE BALL GAME – Band Arrangement
Remind students that they must look through the entire exercise to determine where each auxiliary percussion instrument is used. They should plan accordingly in order to facilitate smooth changes between instruments.

153. SERENGETI (AFRICAN RHAPSODY) – Band Arrangement
This piece is a great exercise of many different percussion sounds contributing to the overall tone quality of a composition. Again, students need to plan where each auxiliary instrument will be located (on trap tables or music stands with carpet or towel) and how they will make smooth changes from one instrument to another.

RUBANK® STUDIES

154. CHORALE
Use long, slow strokes on the Timpani. Vary the speed of the rolls on Suspended Cymbal to make an effective crescendo and decrescendo.

155. CHORALE
Use sixteenth note hand motions for the multiple bounce rolls on Snare Drum and long, slow strokes on the Bass Drum.

156. CHORALE
Remember, striking the bottom leg of the Triangle will produce a sound with more overtones. As students listen to the band, they will hopefully determine that such a sound works best for this chorale.

157. CHORALE
Use long, slow strokes on the Bass Drum part, especially for the dotted half notes in measures 1, 2, and 6.

158. CHORALE
If too much emphasis is placed on the "hairpin" effect in measures 3 and 4, the multiple bounce roll may sound "lumpy" as a result of hearing the individual hand motions (pulsations). Students should concentrate primarily on the quality of the multiple bounce roll, then focus attention on the dynamic effect.

159.
Since the nine-stroke open rolls in this exercise are not preceded by sixteenth note rhythms to establish the hand motions, it is important for students to be thinking about the speed of the hands before they begin to play.

Keyboard Percussion

150. SEMPER FIDELIS – Band Arrangement
Students should select a melodic sticking according to the contour of the melodic line.

151. DANNY BOY – Band Arrangement
Remember to use long, slow strokes especially when playing double stopped whole notes.

152. TAKE ME OUT TO THE BALL GAME – Band Arrangement
Use a light stroke with a faster up-stroke to achieve the style and character of this exercise.

153. SERENGETI (AFRICAN RHAPSODY) – Band Arrangement
Count carefully when it comes to measure repeats; it's very easy to get lost if you lose your concentration. The phrases are marked in a series of measure repeats with a 4 or an 8 to help the player keep their place in the music.

RUBANK® STUDIES

154. CHORALE
Note the gradual crescendo and decrescendo. Remember to use a long, slow stroke for the double stop at the end.

155. CHORALE
The dynamic changes must be planned carefully in this chorale, as they occur more quickly.

156. CHORALE
Because there is less resonance in the upper register of the instrument; it is important to use long, slow strokes on the half notes.

157. CHORALE
Beginning this chorale with a double left sticking pattern will minimize the amount of mallet crossing in the rest of the piece.

158. CHORALE
Careful planning is necessary to produce an acceptable "hairpin" effect during one measure of crescendo followed by one measure of diminuendo. Use height-of-rise to control the dynamic changes.

159.
Alternate Sticking with a left hand lead is suggested for this exercise.

PERCUSSION TIPS (continued)

Percussion

160.
You may need to point out the Flam Paradiddles in measures 1, 2, and 3, and the Flam Accents in the last half of the exercise.

161.
Since the five-stroke open rolls in this exercise are not preceded by sixteenth note rhythms to establish the hand motions, it is important for students to be thinking about the speed of the hands before they begin to play.

162.
Using Alternate Sticking, the sixteenth note triplet rhythms beginning off the beat will be played with the left hand leading, and those beginning on the beat will be played with the right hand leading.

163.
This exercise is a variation of exercise 159. Notice the addition of the Flams in the last half of the exercise.

164.
Students should use individual hand motions to play the double sticking patterns in this exercise. Do not use a double bounce as you would in an open roll.

165.
You may need to point out the Flamacue in measure 4.

166.
This exercise is a variation of exercise 162. Notice that five-stroke open rolls have replaceîed the sixteenth note triplet rhythms.

167.
This exercise is a variation of exercises 159 and 163. Notice the addition of Flams as well as Double Paradiddles and Paradiddles.

168.
This exercise is a variation of exercise 160. Notice the use of the five- and nine-stroke open rolls in place of the Flam Paradiddles and Flam Accents.

169.
This exercise is a variation of exercise 165. Notice the use of the nine-stroke open rolls in place of the sixteenth notes and Flamacue.

170.
This exercise is a variation of exercise 162. Notice the additional sixteenth note triplet rhythms.

171.
This exercise is a variation of exercise 167. Notice the substitution of the Triple Paradiddle in measure 3 and the addition of the five-stroke open rolls in measure 5.

172.
This exercise is a variation of exercise 160 for the Bass Drum.

Keyboard Percussion

160.
Alternate Sticking with a right hand lead is suggested for this exercise.

161.
Alternate Sticking with a left hand lead is suggested for this exercise.

162.
Alternate Sticking with a right hand lead is suggested for this exercise.

163.
Alternate Sticking with a left hand lead is suggested for this exercise.

164.
Alternate Sticking with a right hand lead is suggested for this exercise.

165.
Alternate Sticking with a left hand lead is suggested for this exercise.

166.
Alternate Sticking with a right hand lead is suggested for this exercise.

167.
Alternate Sticking with a left hand lead is suggested for this exercise.

168.
Alternate Sticking with a right hand lead is suggested for this exercise.

169.
Alternate Sticking with a left hand lead is suggested for this exercise.

170.
Alternate Sticking with a right hand lead is suggested for this exercise.

171.
Alternate Sticking with a left hand lead is suggested for this exercise.

172.
Alternate Sticking with a right hand lead is suggested for this exercise.

PERCUSSION TIPS (continued)

Percussion	Keyboard Percussion

Percussion

173.
This exercise is a variation of exercise 169. Notice the use of additional nine-stroke open rolls as well as the five-stroke open roll at the end.

174.
This exercise is a variation of exercise 170. Notice the substitution of nine-stroke open rolls for the sixteenth note triplet rhythms.

175.
This exercise is a variation of 171. Notice the substitution of the seventeen-stroke open roll for the Paradiddles in measure 3, and the substitution of the nine-stroke open rolls in measure 4.

176.
This exercise is a variation of exercise 172. Notice the use of the seventeen-stroke open rolls in the first half, and the thirteen-stroke open rolls in the second half.

177.
This exercise is a variation of exercise 161. Notice the use of the thirteen-stroke open rolls throughout the piece.

178.
This exercise is a variation of exercise 170. Notice the use of the additional sixteenth note triplet rhythms.

179.
As the studies shift from major to minor in the wind and brass parts, the emphasis shifts from measured open rolls to the use of multiple bounce rolls.

180.
Remind students to use two sixteenth note hand motions to play the eighth note multiple bounce rolls, and four sixteenth note hand motions to play the quarter note multiple bounce rolls at the end of each phrase.

181.
Strive to achieve a multiple bounce roll sound that does not have audible pulsations by connecting the sixteenth note hand motions as smoothly as possible.

182.
Students playing the Snare Drum part should listen carefully to the rhythms in the Bass Drum part for good ensemble precision.

183.
Strive to achieve a multiple bounce roll sound that does not have audible pulsations by connecting the sixteenth note hand motions as smoothly as possible.

184.
Due to the nature of the rhythms in this exercise, the multiple bounce rolls will constantly alternate. Practice these multiple bounce rolls beginning with both left and right hands.

185.
The rhythms of the chromatic scale in the wind and brass parts are wonderfully supported by Flam Accents and triplet-based multiple bounce rolls. Connect the eighth note triplet hand motions as smoothly as possible.

Keyboard Percussion

173.
Alternate Sticking with a left hand lead is suggested for this exercise.

174.
Alternate Sticking with a right hand lead is suggested for this exercise.

175.
Alternate Sticking with a left hand lead is suggested for this exercise.

176.
Alternate Sticking with a right hand lead is suggested for this exercise.

177.
Alternate Sticking with a left hand lead is suggested for this exercise.

178.
Alternate Sticking with a right hand lead is suggested for this exercise.

179.
Alternate Sticking with a left hand lead is suggested for this exercise.

180.
Alternate Sticking with a right hand lead is suggested for this exercise.

181.
Alternate Sticking with a left hand lead is suggested for this exercise.

182.
Alternate Sticking with a right hand lead is suggested for this exercise.

183.
Alternate Sticking with a left hand lead is suggested for this exercise.

184.
Alternate Sticking with a right hand lead is suggested for this exercise.

185.
Alternate Sticking with a right hand lead is suggested for this exercise.

Percussion

186.
In this exercise, the multiple bounce rolls are preceded by the correct number of eighth note triplet hand motions.

INDIVIDUAL STUDY - KEYBOARD PERCUSSION

187.
The next four exercises are designed to develop the smooth, connected multiple bounce rolls used by mature percussionists to completely fill the space at certain tempos. Begin by playing the sixteenth note triplet rhythms at the end of each measure, then substitute smooth multiple bounce strokes using the sixteenth note triplet hand motions. The rolls will begin with the left hand.

188.
By adding an additional set of sixteenth note triplets, the multiple bounce roll is now extended to one full beat. The rolls in this exercise begin with the right hand.

189.
Next, another additional set of sixteenth note triplets is added, thus extending the multiple bounce roll to one and one-half beats. The rolls in this exercise begin with the left hand.

190.
Finally, a fourth set of sixteenth note triplets is added to the pattern, which extends the multiple bounce roll to a total of two full beats. The rolls in this exercise begin with the right hand. These four exercises should be practiced daily.

191.
Using Natural Sticking (as indicated) will produce a smooth, flowing pattern that has a good feel in the hands.

192.
This exercise is a more advanced combination of Flam rudiments which is designed to improve individual technique.

193.
All of these measured open rolls are based on sixteenth note hand motions. The rolls will alternate, so practice each roll individually with both left and right hands leading. Strive for an even, connected sound without pulsations.

194.
All of these measured open rolls are also based on sixteenth note hand motions, but will be played with the same hand throughout the exercise. Nevertheless, practice all of these rolls right-handed as well as left-handed.

195.
This short etude features different note lengths (which require a variety of stroke lengths), staccato articulations, accents, and dynamic contrasts. Have students concentrate on one element at a time, and then combine the elements as they become more comfortable with the etude. Students should listen carefully to the accompaniment track when they practice with the CD.

Keyboard Percussion

186.
Alternate Sticking with a right hand lead is suggested for this exercise.

INDIVIDUAL STUDY - KEYBOARD PERCUSSION

187.
Use full legato strokes when practicing this exercise. Alternate Sticking with a right hand lead is suggested.

188.
This arpeggio study is designed to begin on the left hand and continue with Alternate Sticking.

189.
Play the ascending pattern using an Alternate Sticking with a left hand lead. The descending pattern should also use Alternate Sticking, but begin with the right hand.

190.
To Double Stick at faster tempos, it is important to achieve a good height-of-rise.

191.
Use long, slow strokes to practice these octaves.

192.
Legato Strokes are also applied to this quarter note octave scale pattern.

193.
Use Alternate Sticking with a right hand lead for this chromatic scale exercise.

194.
If Alternate Sticking is applied to this exercise, begin measures 1 and 3 with the left hand, and measures 2 and 4 with the right hand.

195.
Begin each five-note group with the same hand, then use an Alternate Sticking pattern.

PERCUSSION TIPS (continued)

Percussion

196.
This short etude also features different note lengths (which require a variety of stroke lengths) and dynamic contrasts. Have students review Crash Cymbal techniques for the most appropriate sound. Students should listen carefully to the accompaniment track when they practice with the CD.

197.
Different performance techniques and dynamic contrasts are found in this etude. Have students decide how they are going to play the Tambourine for the most appropriate sound.
• Soft, light sounds–use one or two fingers near the edge of the head.
• Medium loud sounds–use the tips of all fingers one-third of the way from the edge to the center.
• Loud sounds–use the knuckles on the head, half-way between the edge and the center.
Encourage students to listen carefully to the accompaniment track when they practice with the CD.

198.
This short etude also features different note lengths and dynamic contrasts. Have students decide where they are going to play the Triangle (bottom leg or leg opposite the open end) for the most appropriate sound. During practice, listening carefully to the accompaniment track on the CD can be very helpful.

199.
This short etude features different note lengths (which require a variety of stroke lengths), staccato and legato articulations, and dynamic contrasts. Have students concentrate on one element at a time, and then combine the elements as they become more comfortable with the etude. The accompaniment track on the CD can be very useful if listened to carefully during practice.

200. ACCENT ARTICULATO – Snare Drum Solo (Unaccompanied)
This Snare Drum solo was composed in a style appropriate for use in a solo/ensemble contest. It represents a culmination of additional techniques learned in Essential Elements 2000. Students have the option of using different sticking systems (Alternate, Right Hand Lead, Paradiddle) for the opening theme (which returns in measure 29). The eighth note triplet patterns beginning in measure 17 (and again in measure 37) should be played using Alternate Sticking.

201. STRAIGHT SIX EIGHT – Snare Drum Solo (Unaccompanied)
This Snare Drum solo was composed in a style appropriate for use in a solo/ensemble contest. It represents a culmination of many of the techniques learned in Essential Elements 2000. Note the difference between the open rolls (played with eighth note hand motions) and the multiple bounce rolls (also played with eighth note hand motions). The Paratriplets in measures 25-26 (and again in measures 29-30) are simply Paradiddles applied to the 6/8 meter. Use Alternate Sticking from measure 49 to the end. Two different performance tempos have been selected for the CD track to assist in the development of this solo piece.

Keyboard Percussion

196.
The Right Hand Lead sticking system works well with this exercise.

197.
Alternate Sticking with a right hand lead is suggested for this exercise.

198.
Alternate Sticking is suggested for this exercise; students may begin with either hand.

199.
This sticking challenge features Double Sticking patterns within each measure as well as over the bar line. This is a great exercise for developing overall technique.

200. INTERMEZZO from "CARMEN" – Orchestra Bells Solo
This solo was arranged for Orchestra Bells in a style appropriate for use in a solo/ensemble contest. It allows the opportunity to use the Legato Stroke approach on the instrument to produce a smooth, flowing musical line. Care should be taken to use a longer, slower stroke on the octaves at the end followed by a light, short up-stroke for the last note.

201. GYPSY DANCE from "CARMEN" – Xylophone Solo
This solo was arranged for Xylophone in a style appropriate for use in a solo/ensemble contest. It allows the opportunity to use an approach with a lighter stroke (faster up-stroke) to produce a flowing musical line. Dynamic contrasts are an important part of this piece as are the releases of the rolled notes.

Authors

DR. TIM LAUTZENHEISER
Founder, Attitude Concepts For Today, Bluffton, IN

JOHN HIGGINS
Managing Producer and Editor, Composer and Arranger, Hal Leonard Corp., Milwaukee, WI

CHARLES T. MENGHINI, D.M.A.
Director of Bands and Dean, Undergraduate Division; VanderCook College of Music, Chicago, IL

PAUL LAVENDER
Vice President – Instrumental Publications, Composer and Arranger, Hal Leonard Corp., Milwaukee, WI

TOM C. RHODES
President, RBC Music Inc., San Antonio, TX

DON BIERSCHENK
Vice President, RBC Music Inc., San Antonio, TX

Credits

Managing Editor and Producer	Paul Lavender
Production Editors	Stuart Malavsky Darlene Kaminski
Full Band Arrangements	John Higgins
Percussion Consultant and Editor	Will Rapp
Design and Art Direction	Richard Slater Tim Begonia
Music Engraving and Typesetting	Thomas Schaller
Assistant to Authors	Darcy Davis
Play Along Trax Arrangements and Production	Paul Lavender John Higgins
Additional Arrangements	John Moss
Individual Study Arrangements	Paul Lavender John Higgins Steve Potts
Essential Elements Rhythm Section	Steve Millikan - Keyboards Steve Dokken - Bass Sandy Williams - Guitars Steve Hanna - Percussion Larry Sauer - Drums
Individual Study Accompaniment Recordings	Steve Potts - Piano
Recording and Mixing Engineers Aire Born Studios, Indianapolis, IN	Mark Aspinall John Bolt David Price Ben Vawter
Additional Recording Production	Jared Rodin Mark Aspinall
Project Supervision Aire Born Studios, Indianapolis, IN	Nanci Milam Mike Wilson Nina Hunt
Announcer	Scott Hoke

Featured Instrumental Artists

Flute	Robin Peller Indianapolis Symphony Orchestra
Oboe	Roger Roe Indianapolis Symphony Orchestra
Bassoon	Robert Broemel Principal, Indianapolis Symphony Orchestra
Clarinet, Alto Clarinet, Bass Clarinet	Michael Borschel Indianapolis Symphony Orchestra
Alto, Tenor, and Baritone Saxophones	John Hibler Free lance performer and recording artist
Trumpet	Robert L. Wood Indianapolis Symphony Orchestra
Horn	Gerald Montgomery Indianapolis Symphony Orchestra
Trombone, Baritone	K. Blake Schlabach Indianapolis Symphony Orchestra
Tuba	Anthony Kniffen Principal, Indianapolis Symphony Orchestra
Electric Bass	Steve Dokken Free lance performer and recording artist
Percussion	Steve Hanna Free lance performer and recording artist, Applied Percussion, DePauw University
Percussion	Will Rapp, D.M.A. Director of Bands and Applied Percussion, Kutztown University, PA

The authors wish to give special thanks to Herman Knoll, Senior Vice President of Hal Leonard, for his dedication, leadership, and expertise in the creation of the Essential Elements educational program.